RESUMES *that* KNOCK 'EM 'EM DEAD

by Martin John Yate

Martin John Yate, one of today's foremost career authorities, is the author of *Knock 'em Dead With Great Answers To Tough Interview Questions,* the popular interview guide published in numerous foreign versions, as well as the new third edition here in the United States. Mr. Yate, who is also a syndicated feature writer and employment/management lecturer, was born and educated in England. He served as Director of Personnel for Bell Industries Computer Memory Division and then as Director of Training for the Dunhill Personnel System, one of the largest personnel services organizations in the country. Currently, he is a special training consultant to some of the leading companies in the employment services industry and the corporate world.

This book, Mr. Yate's third, follows his successful title *Hiring The Best: A Manager's Guide To Effective Interviewing.* In *Resumes That Knock 'em Dead,* the author provides authoritative advice on the troublesome—but essential—professional task of composing a resume. The book is the result of over a year's worth of planning and research, in addition to countless hours of interviews with the nation's top personnel, management, and employment specialists.

Acknowledgments

It is only fair to say that any book is teamwork, and this one more than most.

I would like to thank three people especially: Donna Carnavale; my editor, Eric Blume, who continues his inestimable contributions in this, our third book together; and Jeff Hunter, a man with a superior talent, and the president of First Impressions, a truly top-notch resume-writing firm.

Also by Martin John Yate:

Knock 'em Dead with Great Answers to
Tough Interview Questions

Hiring the Best: A Manager's Guide to
Effective Interviewing

Published by
Bob Adams, Inc.
260 Center Street
Holbrook, MA 02343

ISBN: 1-55850-955-0

Manufactured in the United States of America.

Contents

Chapter Nine:
The Resumes / 71

Based on real resumes that got real jobs for real people. Which jobs? In alphabetical order:

Accountant
Accounting Customer Service Specialist
Accounting Clerk
Accounts Payable Supervisor
Administrative Assistant
Admissions Representative
Applications Management Specialist
Applications Programmer/Analyst
Assistant Manager Trainee
Associate(Legal)
Automobile Salesperson
Automotive Management Specialist
Bank Teller
Bank Wire Transfer Clerk
Banking Portfolio Manager
Bookkeeper
Broadcast Management Professional
Buyer
Capital Equipment Salesperson
Chemical Salesperson
Claims Representative
Compensation/EEO Specialist
Commercial Lender
Computer Operator
Credit/Collections Clerk
Credit/Loan Supervisor
Credit Manager
Customer Service Manager
Data Processing Consultant
Data Processing Supervisor
Database Administrator
Dietitian
Director of Development
Director of Medical Records
Electrical Design Engineer
Electrician
Engineering Secretary
Executive Assistant
Fabric Salesperson
Field Sales Manager
Financial Executive Secretary
Food and Beverage Director
Food Product Manager
Food Service Salesperson
Health Care Professional
Health Care Sales Manager
High Tech Sales Manager
High Tech Salesperson
Hospital Pharmacist
Inventory Control Buyer
Junior Accounting Clerk
Law Clerk
Lease Accountant
Legal Office Manager

Legal Secretary
Major Account Executive
Manufacturing Systems Engineer
Marketing Analyst
Mechanical Engineer
Medical Equipment Salesperson
Medical Goods Sales Manager
Microcomputer Support Analyst
Neonatal Support/Nurse
Occupational Therapist
Office Administrator
Office Manager
Operating Room Services Specialist
Operations Management Specialist
Order Processing Manager
Paralegal
Payroll/Accounts Payable Supervisor
Personnel Administrator
Personnel Assistant
Physical Therapist
Plastics Engineer
Process Control Engineer
Product Development Engineer
Project Leader
Programmer Analyst
Public Relations/Media Spokesperson
Publishing/Marketing Professional
Quality Control Manager
Real Estate Professional
Real Estate Sales Manager
Receptionist
Records Manager
Research Scientist
Sales Manager
Sales Support/Administration Specialist
Salesperson
Senior Executive Secretary
Senior Payroll Clerk
Senior Systems Programmer
Software Engineer
Staff Accountant/Real Estate
Store Manager
Systems Programmer
Systems Team Leader
Technical Services Manager
Telecommunications Analyst
Textile Designer/Stylist
Ultrasound/Nuclear Medicine Technician
Underwriting Typist
Veterinary Intern
Visual Merchandising Specialist
Wholesale Electrical Sales
Word Processing Specialist
Word Processing Supervisor

Appendix / 195

Resumes for Special Situations; Off The Beaten Track; For More Help...; Sample Questionnaire

Introduction

Most of the books on writing resumes haven't changed to accommodate today's dynamic work environment. That is the reason for this book: To help "now" people get the very best jobs!

Look at the other resume books on the market; they are full of resume examples with dates going back to what seems, to most job seekers, like the Bronze Age. They use job titles that no longer exist and techniques that no longer work—techniques that in many instances can be downright damaging to your job hunt.

This book is unique in two very important ways.

First, you'll get to read real resumes from real people. Each of the resumes in this book is based on a "genuine article" that worked wonders for its writer. Included are resumes from today's, and tomorrow's, in-demand jobs, as defined by the Bureau of Labor Statistics and confirmed by the professionals on the front lines: Corporate recruiters and other employment industry professionals across the country. The odds are that you are already working in one of these jobs, or wishing you were.

Also included in the "real-life" section of this book is a selection of resumes from people with special challenges. These reflect the pressures and needs of a modern, professionally-oriented society struggling into the information age. Like the resume that got a six-dollar-an-hour factory worker a $70,000 a year job; or the one that helped a recovering alcoholic and drug-abuser get back on her feet again. There are winning resumes of people recovering from serious emotional challenges, mental problems, re-entering society after jail, starting over after divorce, changing careers, and even one for a teenage trick cyclist looking for advertising, film, and endorsement work. And what's more, these examples have proved themselves effective in every corner of the nation; the writers landed both interviews and jobs.

Second, I explain the ins and outs of putting a resume together as painlessly as possible. I'll show you the three best ways to look at your background and present your resume. Then I'll show you all the available options for inclusion. Why certain things should be in your resume, how they should look, and why other things should never appear. Wherever industry experts disagree, I'll give you both sides of the argument, and my reasoned solution to the dispute. That way, you can make a prudent decision about your unique background, based on possession of all the facts and the best advice going. In addition, you will see the infinite variety of styles and approaches that can be used within my guidelines, to help you create a truly individual resume.

These two unique concepts, the numerous resume examples, and the nuts-and-bolts sections about resume production and distribution give you everything needed to create a distinctive, professional resume: one that will Knock 'em Dead.

Chapter One: The Marks of a Great Resume

Who needs a resume?

Everyone. Certainly you do, unless you are so well known that your reputation is already common knowledge to all potential employers. If that were the case you probably wouldn't be reading this book in the first place.

Anyone, in any job, can be viewed more favorably than his or her competition - if he or she is better organized and prepared, which is what a good resume demonstrates. It's a staunch friend who only speaks well of you and can gain you entrance into undreamed of opportunities.

Now, no resume ever gets carefully read unless a manager is trying to solve a problem. That problem may be finding a quicker way to manufacture silicon chips. It may be getting the telephone calls answered, now that the receptionist has left. As disparate as these examples might seem, both are still concerned with problem solving. And invariably, the problem that needs a solution is the same: Productivity. The simple question, "How on earth are we going to get things done quicker/cheaper/more efficiently without a _____?".

Resumes that get acted upon are those that demonstrate the writer's potential as a problem-solver.

Your resume must speak loudly and clearly of your value as a potential employee. And the value must be spoken in a few brief seconds, because in the business world, that's all the attention a resume will get. The resume takes you only the first few paces toward that new job. It gets your foot in the door, and because you can't be there to answer questions, it has to stand on its own.

A resume's emphasis is on what has happened in your business life, what actions you took to make those things happen, and what supportive personal characteristics you brought to the job. It is about how you contributed to solving a business' problems. It has nothing to do with generalizations or personal opinions.

The resume itself came about as a solution to a problem: How does a manager avoid interviewing every applicant who applies for a job? Can you imagine what would happen to a business if everyone who applied for a job was given even a cursory ten-minute interview? The company would simply grind to a halt, then topple into bankruptcy. The solution: Come up with a way to get a glimpse of applicants' potential before having to meet them face-to-face. The resume appeared and evolved into an important screening and time-saving tool.

While that solved one problem for the employer, it created another for the job applicant: "Considering that my background isn't perfect, how do I write a resume that shows off my best potential?" The first attempt to answer that question is how the gentle art of resume writing came into being.

In the world of recreational reading, resumes are pretty far down on the list. They are usually deadly dull and offer little competition to murder mysteries, tales of international intrigue, and love stories.

Nevertheless, resumes are a required part of every manager's daily reading, and exactly because they are usually deadly dull, are generally avoided. To combat this deep-seated avoidance, there is a general rule that will help your resume get read and acted upon in the quickest possible time: It needs to be short and long. Short on words, but long on facts and an energy that reflects the real you.

Good resume writing focuses attention on your strengths and shows you as a potential powerhouse of an employee. At the same time, it draws attention away from those areas that lack definition or vigor. You can do this even if you are changing your entire career direction, or starting your life over for other reasons, and I'll show you how.

There is a hidden benefit, too, in the resume writing process: It focuses your attention and helps you prepare for job interviews. In a very real sense, putting a resume together is the foundation of succeeding at the job interview. Preparation for one is preparation for the other.

For example, the interviewer's command to "tell me about yourself" is one of those tough interview demands that almost all of us have difficulty answering satisfactorily. Were you totally satisfied with your response last time it came up? I doubt it. You can only answer it well if you have taken the time to analyze and package all your strengths and weaknesses in an organized fashion. It is the only way you will ever learn to speak fluidly about your background and skills in a fashion guaranteed to impress the interviewer. So, why not kill two birds with one stone—prepare for the interview by preparing a resume that will open all the right doors for you.

Interestingly enough, the majority of interviewers accept the contents of a resume as fact. Additionally, a good number of interviewers base all their questions on the resume content: This means that in a very real way you can plan and guide the course of the majority of your interviews by preparing an effective resume.

Those without resumes are forced to reveal their history on a job application form, which does not always allow the perfect representation of skills, and which gives the interviewer no flattering starting point from which to base the interview questions.

In addition to helping you get your foot in the door and easing the course of the interview, your resume will be your last and most powerful advocate. After all the interviewing of all the candidates is done, how do you think the interviewers review and evaluate all the contenders? They go over their notes, application forms, and the resumes supplied by the job candidates. You will want to make it something powerful and positive.

Finally, the preparation of a good resume has the broad, intangible benefit of personal discovery. You may find, as you answer some of the questions in Chapter Four, that your experience is deeper than you imagined, that your contributions to previous employers were more important that you thought. You may look on your career direction in a new light. And you may see your value as a solid employee increase. You will gain confidence that will be important for not only a good performance at the interview, but your attitude toward the rest of your career.

No sane person will tell you that resume writing is fun, but I will show you the tricks of the trade, developed over the years by executive recruiters and professional resume writers, that make the process easier.

What makes this book truly different is that the resume examples in it are all real resumes from real people, resumes that recently landed them real jobs in "in-demand" professions. They were all sent to me by employment specialists from around the nation. For example, the healthcare examples were screened initially by professional healthcare recruiters, those in data processing by computer recruiters. And these are the pros on the firing line, who know what works and what doesn't in today's business marketplace.

You will find everything you need to make resume writing fast, effective, and painless. Just follow my instructions, and in a few hours you'll have a knock-out resume and never have to read another word about the damn things as long as you live. With that in mind, do it once and do it right—you'll generate a top-flight resume without knocking yourself out!

So now, for your delight and edification, we'll review the marks of a great resume: What type of resume is right for you, what always goes in (and why), what always stays out (and why), and what might go in depending on your special circumstances. This is followed by countless resume examples and a "painting-by-numbers" guide that makes resume writing easy for anyone!

With the changing times and circumstances, there are few rigid rules for every situation. So in those instances where there are exceptions, I'll explain them and your choices. The judgment call will be yours. And when you are finished, you will have one of the very best resumes, one that will be sure to knock 'em dead.

Chapter Two: Three Ways to Sum Yourself Up

"Give me a moment of your busy day! Listen to me, I got something to say!" That's what your resume must scream—in a suitably professional manner, of course. *Not* in the manner of the would-be retail clothing executive who had his resume "hand-delivered". . . attached to the hand and arm of a store window mannequin.

As it happened, that was only the first surprise in store for the personnel director who received the delivery: The envelope was hand-decorated in gothic script; the cover letter inside was equally decorative (and illegible); the resume writer had glued the four-page resume to fabric, and stitched the whole mess together like a child's book. The crowning glory, however, was yet to come: All the punctuation marks—commas, colons, periods and the like—were small rhinestone settings. Yes, it got noticed, but its success had to depend entirely on the recipient's sense of humor—which in this case was most noticeable in its absence.

Here's the point: trying do something out of the ordinary with any aspect of your resume is risky business indeed. For every interview door it opens, at least two more will be slammed shut.

The best (and most business-like) bet is to present a logically displayed, eye-appealing resume that will get *read*. That means grabbing the reader right away—on that first page. And that's one big reason for short, power-packed resumes.

We all have different backgrounds. Some of us have worked for one company only, some of us have worked for eleven companies in as many years. Some of us have changed careers once or twice, some of us have maintained a predictable career path. For some, diversity broadens our potential, and for some concentration deepens it. We each require different vehicles to put our work history in the most exciting light. The goals, though, are constant:

- To show off achievements, attributes, and cumulation of expertise to the best advantage.

- To minimize any possible weaknesses.

Resume experts acknowledge just three essential styles for presenting your credentials to a potential employer: Chronological, Functional, and Combination (Chrono-Functional). Your particular circumstances will determine the right format for you. Just three styles, you say? You will see resume books with up to fifteen varieties of resume style. Such volumes are, alas, merely filling up space; in the final analysis, each additional style such books mention is a tiny variation on the above three.

The Chronological Resume

This is the most common and readily accepted form of presentation. It's what most of us think of when we think of resumes—a chronological listing of job titles and responsibilities. It starts with the current or most recent employment, then works backwards to your first job (or ten years into the past—whichever comes first).

This format is good for demonstrating your growth in a single profession. It is suitable for anyone with practical work experience who hasn't suffered too many job changes or prolonged periods of unemployment. It is not suitable if you are just out of school or if you are changing careers. The format would then draw attention to your weaknesses (i.e., your lack of specific experience in a field) rather than your strengths.

The exact content of every resume naturally varies depending on individual circumstances. A chronological resume usually incorporates six basic components.

- *Contact Information*

- *A Job Objective*

- *A Career Objective*

- *A Career Summary*

- *Education*

- *A Description of Work History*

This last item is the distinguishing characteristic of the chronological resume, because it ties your job responsibilities and achievements to specific employers, job titles, and dates.

There are also some optional categories determined by the space available to you and the unique aspects of your background. You will see these in Chapter Three.

The Functional Resume

This format focuses on the professional skills you have developed over the years, rather than when, where or how you acquired them. It de-emphasizes dates, sometimes to the point of exclusion. By the same token, job titles and employers play a minor part with this type of resume. The attention is always focused on the skill rather than the context or time of its acquisition.

In many ways, the content of the functional resume is similar to the chronological type. Only the approach is different. It is a case not so much of what you say, but of how you say it.

This functional format is suited to a number of different personal circumstances, specifically those of:

- Mature professionals with a storehouse of expertise and jobs;

- Entry-level types whose track records do not justify a chronological resume;

- Career-changers who want to focus on skills rather than credentials;

- People whose careers have been stagnant or in ebb, who want to give focus to the skills that can get a career under way again, rather than on the history in which it was becalmed in the first place;

- Military personnel embarking on a civilian career;

- Those returning to the workplace after a long absence;

- People closer to retirement than to the onset of their careers.

The functional resume does present a major challenge for the writer. Because it focuses so strongly on skills and ability to contribute in a particular direction, you must have an employment objective clearly in mind. When this is achieved, such a resume can be very effective. Without this focus, however, or if you are looking for "a job, any job," this format loses its direction and tends to drift without purpose.

Though a functional resume is a bit more free-form than a chronological one, there are certain essentials that make it work. In addition to contact information and a job and/or career objective, these would include the elements listed below.

- *A Functional Summary.* Different skills are needed for different jobs, so the functional summary is where you make the tough decisions to determine what goes in and what stays out. Consider the case of an executive sales secretary bored with her job but challenged by the excitement and money the sales force is enjoying. She will want to emphasize those abilities that lead to success in sales, such as written and verbal communication skills, and time management. On the other hand, she will almost certainly leave out references to her typing and short-hand abilities, because these skills no longer contribute to her new goals.

- *Dates.* Strictly speaking, a functional resume needn't give dates. Up until a couple of years ago, you could still sometimes get away with omitting them. That is no longer the case. Today, a resume without dates waves a big red flag at every employer in the land. So, what if your employment history doesn't have all the stability it might? The functional resume is perfect for you, because dates can be de-emphasized by their placement. You put them at the end of the resume, or perhaps on a second page, for example, in a small block of type; and you use year dates omitting the details of day, week, and month. The idea is to force the reader's attention to your skills, not your history.

- *Education.* The inclusion of education and other optional categories, determined by the space available to you and the unique aspects of your background. As I pointed out a little earlier, you will see them in Chapter Three.

The Combination Chrono-Functional Resume

For the upwardly mobile professional with a track record, this is becoming the resume of choice. It has all the flexibility and strength that come from combining both the chronological and functional formats. If you have a performance record, and are on a career track and want to pursue it, then this is the strongest resume tool available. This format, in addition to contact information and a job objective, incorporates a number of identifying factors, outlined below.

- *A Career Summary.* The combination resume, more often than not, has some kind of career summary. Here you spotlight a professional with a clear sense of self, a past of solid contributions, and a clear focus on future career growth. The career summary, as you might expect, will include a power-packed description of skills, achievements, and personal traits that fairly scream "Success!"

- *A Description of Functional Skills.* This is where the combination of styles comes into play. Following the summary, the combination resume starts out like a functional resume and highlights achievements in different categories relevant to the job/career goals, without any reference to employers.

- *A Chronological History.* Then it switches to the chronological approach and names companies, dates, titles, duties, and responsibilities. This section can also include further evidence of achievements or special contributions.

- *Education.* Then come the optional categories determined by the space available to you and the unique aspects of your background.

One of these styles is perfect for you. Pick one, and in the next chapter we'll begin to fill it in with the resume basics.

Chapter Three: The Basic Ingredients

It used to be that there were just a few set rules for writing a great resume. Everything was simple—you did this, you didn't do that. Now, however, many of the jobs for which those rules were made no longer exist—so many of the traditional hard and fast rules no longer apply. New technologies are creating new professions overnight, and, with them, new career opportunities. The content of these new professions and careers is dramatically different from the employment world of a few short years ago. Times and the rules of the game have changed, and these changes require that we adopt a modern and flexible approach to resume writing.

What used to be strictly off-limits in all resumes is now acceptable in many and required in some (the need for technical jargon to explain skills, for example, comes to mind). Elements that were once always included, such as the mug shot, are now frowned upon in almost every instance. And so it goes on; creating a fog of confusion for everyone. What are the rules?

Today, writing a resume can be likened to baking a cake. In most instances, the ingredients are essentially the same. What determines the flavor is the order and quantity in which those ingredients are blended. There are certain ingredients that go into almost every resume. There are others that rarely or never go in, and there are those special touches that are added (a pinch of this, a dash of that), depending on your personal tastes and requirements.

Sound complicated? It really isn't. This chapter will explain it all. If a certain ingredient must always go in, you will understand why; the same goes for something that should never appear in your resume. In circumstances where the business world holds conflicting views, these views will be explained so that a reasoned judgment can be made. In these instances you will always get my reasoned opinion, based on my extensive experience and contact in the human resources field.

First, let's look at the ingredients that are part of the mix of every successful resume.

What Must Always Go In

Name

We start with the obvious, but there are other considerations about your name besides remembering to put it on your resume. Give your first and last name only. It isn't necessary to include your middle name(s). My name is Martin John Yate—it says so on all my books—but my resume says simply Martin Yate, because that is the way I would introduce myself in person. Notice also that it isn't M. J. Yate, because that

13

would force the reader to play Twenty Questions about the meaning of my initials, and the average resume reader isn't looking for light entertainment. Even if you are known by your initials—like that chap B.J. on *M*A*S*H* or J.R. on *Dallas*—don't put it on your resume. If you use quotation marks or parentheses, those on the receiving end might think it a little strange. Better that it come out at the interview when the interviewer asks you what you like to be called: At the very least, you'll have some small talk to break the tense interview atmosphere.

It is not required to place Mr., Ms., Miss, Mrs. before your name. But what if your first name is Gayle, Carrol, Leslie, or any of the other names that can easily be used for members of either sex? While it isn't strictly necessary, in such instances it is acceptable to put Mr. Gayle Jones, or Ms. Leslie Jackson. The reasoning is based on human frailty and the ever-present foot-in-mouth syndrome: In contacting you to follow up on your resume, your interviewer is likely to make the mistake of asking to speak to Ms. Gayle Jones, or Mr. Leslie Jackson. Though it is a little mistake that is easily corrected, the possible future employer is immediately put in the awkward position of starting the relationship with an apology. If your name falls into the "genderless" category, avoid the complication and employ a title.

Finally, for those who are the IInd, IIIrd, Junior or Senior holders of their name: If you always add "Jr." or "III" when you sign your name or if that is the way you are addressed to avoid confusion, go ahead and use it. Otherwise, it is extraneous information on the resume, and therefore not needed.

Address

Always give your complete address. Do not abbreviate unless space restrictions make it absolutely mandatory—you want the post office to have every possible advantage when it comes to delivering those offer letters efficiently. If you do abbreviate—such as St. or Apt.—be consistent. The state of your residence, however, is always abbreviated to two capitalized letters (for example, MN, WV, LA), according to post office standards. Always include the correct zip code.

The accepted format for laying out your address looks like this:

Maxwell Krieger
2 Caswell Place, Apartment 38
New York, NY 23456

Notice that the city, state and zip code all go on the same line, with a comma between city and state.

Telephone Number

Always include your telephone number: Few businesses will send you an invitation for an interview in the mail. Including your area code is important even if you have no intention of leaving the area. In this era of decentralization, your resume might end up being screened in another part of the country altogether!
Examples:

(202)555-5555
202/555-5555

The inclusion or exclusion of a work telephone number is a little bit more of a problem.

The case for inclusion: Featuring your daytime contact number allows prospective employers to reach you at a time of their convenience.

The case for exclusion: Being pulled out of the Monday meeting every five minutes to take calls from headhunters and Fortune 500 executives can ruin your whole day. The funny thing about employers is that they always prefer to lose you at their convenience rather than yours. In addition, keeping the company number off the resume adds to its life expectancy. Who needs another detail that may be obsolete in short order?

The solution: Unless your current employer knows of your job search, leave the business number off the resume, but put it in your cover letter. Good cover letters do this with a short sentence that conveys the information and demonstrates you as a responsible employee. For example, something like this can work very well:

"I prefer not to use my employer's time taking personal calls at work, but with discretion you can reach me at 202/555-5555, extension 555, to initiate contact."

Job Objective

This section sometimes appears on resumes as

Position Desired

Job Objective

Objective

Employment Objective

All are acceptable. Regardless of the heading, the job objective has traditionally meant one or two sentences about the kind of job you want and what you can contribute to the company in return for such a job. You will recall from Chapter Two that the use of a job objective in your resume will depend in part on the style of resume you employ to present your qualifications. Remember that the functional resume in particular almost demands one.

That notwithstanding, feelings run strong about whether or not to include a job objective in the resume, so let's review the cases for and against, then reach a considered conclusion.

The case for inclusion: Without a job objective, a resume can have no focus, no sense of direction. And if you don't know where you are going, you can't write a resume, because the body copy has nothing to support. The resume revolves around your objective like the earth around the sun.

The case for exclusion: A job objective is too constricting and can exclude you from consideration from countless jobs you might have been interested in, and for which you are qualified. And after creating a resume with the intent of opening as many doors as possible, you wouldn't want to have half of them slammed shut. Besides, employers are not generally believed to be overly concerned about what you want from them until they have a damn good idea about what they can get out of you.

The solution: You do need an objective, but it needn't fit the traditional definition. The best resumes have objectives written in broad, non-specific terms. They are often little more than a categorization, such as:

Job Objective: Marketing Management

Sometimes, these objectives appear at the top of a resume, as a headline and attention-grabber. If they go beyond that, they focus on skills, achievements and relevant personal characteristics that support the argument.

Job Objective: To pursue an accounting career.

STAFF ACCOUNTANT—REAL ESTATE
To obtain a responsible position in a company where my experience, accomplishments, and proficiency will allow me the opportunity for growth.

This last approach is best, because it considers the forces at work in business these days. Including Job Objectives has as much to do with filing and retrieval systems and computers as it does with people. On the one hand, the resume-reader is looking for a problem-solver, so, by seeing that you fit into a general area, will want to rush on to the rest of the resume (where there are more specifics). Then what happens? In the best case scenario, you will get a frantic call asking you to state your terms and a start date right away. But what happens when there isn't a need for your particular talents that day? Your resume gets filed or logged onto the company's database. The folks who file resumes aren't rocket scientists, just overworked functionaries trying to dispose of a neverending flow of paper. They want to get rid of it as quickly as possible, so they will file your resume according to your instructions. And unless you give it the right help, it may not be filed under the right category; it may never see the light of day again. The broader your objective, the greater frequency with which it will be retrieved and reviewed in the future.

The same argument holds true for resumes sent to employment agencies and executive recruiters, who have been known to keep them on file for as long as ten years.

Just recently, in fact, I heard one of those wonderful tales of an eight-year-old resume that landed a job for its writer, because it had a general objective. Why is this relevant? Had the specific job objective of an entry-level professional been on that resume, the writer would never have been considered.

Such considerations are encouraging many job seekers to include brief and nonspecific job objectives in their resumes. You will learn how to come up with the right tone for your specific needs later in the book.

Employment Dates

Resume readers are often leery of resumes without employment dates. If you expect a response, you can increase your odds dramatically by including them—in one form or another.

With a steady work history and no employment gaps you can can be very specific (space allowing) and write:

January 11th 1986 to July 4th 1988

or

1/11/86 to 7/4/88

or, to be a little less specific:

January 1986-February 1988

But if there are short employment gaps, you can improve the look of things:

1986-1987

instead of

December 12th 1986 - January 23rd 1987

There is no suggestion here that you should lie about your work history, but it is surprising just how many interviewers will be quite satisfied with such dates. There seems to be a myth that everything written on 20-lb. rag paper needs no further inquiry.

While this technique can effectively hide embarrassing employment gaps, and may be enough to get you in for an interview, you should of course be prepared with an adequate answer to questions about your work history once you sit down with the interviewer. Even if such questions are posed, you will have the opportunity to explain yourself—mano a mano, as it were—and that is a distinct improvement over being peremptorily ruled out by some faceless non-entity before you get a chance to speak your piece. The end justifies the means in this case.

Again, if you abbreviate months and years, do so consistently.

Job Titles

The purpose of a job title on your resume is not to reflect exactly what you were called by a particular employer, but rather provide a generic identification that will be understood by as many employers as possible.

A job title should give the employer "something to hang his hat on." So if your current title is "Junior Accountant, Level Three," realize that such internal titling may well bear no relation to the titling of any other company on earth. I remember looking over the personnel roster of a New York bank and learning, to my astonishment, that it had over one hundred systems analysts (the typical number for an outfit this size is about 12). Then I noticed that they had no programmers or programmer analysts. The reasoning that I eventually unearthed was remarkably simple. The human resources department, finding people to be title-conscious in this area, obligingly gave them the titles they wanted. (Another perceived benefit was that it confused the heck out of the raiding headhunters, who got disgusted with systems analysts who couldn't analyze their way out of a wet paper bag!)

This generic approach to job titles also holds true as your job takes you nearer the top of the corporate ladder. The senior executive knows that the higher up the ladder, the more rarefied the air and the fewer the opportunities. After all, a company only has one Controller or one VP of Operations. Again, to avoid painting yourself into a career corner, you can be "specifically vague" with job titles like:

Administrative Assistant

instead of

Secretary

Accountant

instead of

Junior Accountant Level II

17

It is imperative to examine your current *role* at work, rather than relying on your starting or current title. Job titles within companies change much more slowly than the jobs themselves, so a job change can be the opportunity for some to escape stereotyping and the career stagnation that accompanies it. Take the typist hired three years ago, who has now spent two years with a word processor. Such a person could be identified thus:

Word Processor

instead of

Typist

This approach is important because of the way titles and responsibilities vary from company to company. Often, more senior titles and responsibilities are structured around a person's specific talents, especially so outside the Fortune 1000.

There are two situations, however, that don't lend themselves to this technique:

- When you apply for a specific job where you know the title and the responsibilities, and where the position's title is similar but not the same as your own. (Then the exact title sought should be reflected in your resume— as long as you are not being misleading concerning your capabilities.)

- When you apply for a job in certain specific professions, such as health-care. (A brain surgeon wouldn't want to be specifically vague by tagging herself as a Health Aide.)

Company Name

The names of employers should be included. There is no need to include street address or telephone number of past or present employers, although it can be useful to include the city and state. The company will find the complete address on your employment application.

When working for a multiple-division corporation you may want to list the divisional employer: "Bell Industries" might not be enough, so you would perhaps want to add "Computer Memory Division." By the way, it is quite all right to abbreviate words like Corporation (Corp.), Company (Co.), Limited (Ltd.), or Division (Div.). Again, be consistent.

Here is how you might combine the job title and company name and address:

DESIGN ENGINEER.
Bell Industries, Inc., Computer Memory Div., Mountain View, CA.

The information you are supplying is relevant to the reader, but you don't wish it to detract from space useable to sell yourself. If, for instance, you live in a nationally known city, such as Dallas, you need not add "TX".

There is a possible exception to these guidelines. Employed professionals are justified in omitting current employers when their industry has been reduced to a small community of professionals who know, or know of, each other, and where a confidentiality breach is likely to have damaging repercussions. This usually happens to professionals on the higher rungs of the ladder. Of course, if you don't quite fit into this elite category but are still worried about identifying your firm, you are not obliged to list the name of your current employer.

One approach is simply to label a current company in a fashion that has become perfectly acceptable in today's business climate.

A National Retail Chain

An Established Electronics Manufacturer

A Major Commercial Bank

You will notice that usually a company name is followed by a brief description of the business line:

A National Retail Chain: Women and junior fashions and accessories

An Established Electronics Manufacturer producing monolithic memories

This requirement is obviated when the writer can get the company's function into the heading.

A Major Commercial Bank

The writer who can do this saves a line or two of precious space which can be filled with other valuable data.

Responsibilities

This is what is referred to as the meat, or body copy, of the resume, the area where not only your responsibilities are listed, but where your special achievements and other contributions are also highlighted. This is also one of the key areas that sets the truly great resume apart from the rest. This is a crucial part of the resume; it will be dealt with in detail in Chapters Four and Five.

Endorsements

Remember when you got that difficult job finished so quickly? And all the good things the boss said about your work? Well, in a resume you can very effectively quote him, even if the praise wasn't in writing (though of course it is best to quote directly). A line such as "Praised as most innovative and determined manager in the company" can work wonders.

These third party endorsements are not necessary, and they most certainly shouldn't be used to excess. But one or two can be a useful addition to your resume. Such quotes, used sparingly, can be very impressive; overkill can make you sound too self-important and reduce your chances of winning an interview.

Such endorsements become especially effective when the responsibilities have been quantified with facts, numbers, and percentages.

Accreditation and Licenses

Many fields of work require professional licensure or accreditation. If this is the case in your line of work, be sure to list everything necessary. If you are close to a particular accreditation or license (a C.P.A., for example), you would want to list it with information about the status:

Passed all parts of C.P.A. exam, September '89 (expected certification February '90)

Professional Affiliations

Your affiliation with associations and societies dedicated to your field shows your own dedication to your career. Membership is also important for networking, so if you are not currently a member of one of your industry's professional associations, give serious consideration to joining. Note the emphasis on "professional" in the heading. An employer is almost exclusively interested in your professional associations and societies. Omit references to any religious, political or otherwise potentially controversial affiliations. They simply do not belong on a resume; you want yours to reflect a picture of your professional, not your personal, life.

An exception to this rule is in those jobs where a wide circle of acquaintances is regarded as an asset. Some examples would include jobs in public relations, sales, marketing, real estate, and insurance. In that case, include your membership in the Kiwanis or the Royal Lodge of the Raccoons.

By the same token, a seat on the village board, charitable cause involvement, or fundraising work are all activities that show a willingness to involve oneself and can often demonstrate organizational abilities. Space permitting, these are all activities worthy of inclusion because they show you as a sober and responsible member of the community.

These activities become more important as one climbs the corporate ladder of the larger companies. Those firms that take their community responsibilities seriously look for staff who feel and act the same way—an aspect of corporate culture applying itself at the most immediate levels.

Some corporations are committed to the idea that community activities are good public relations. Accordingly, such work may mark an individual for even greater responsibilities and recognition once in the company.

As for method of inclusion, brevity is the rule.

American Heart Association: Area Fundraising Chair

My personal observation is that these activities increase in importance with the maturity of the individual. Employers, quite selfishly perhaps, like to think of their younger staff burning the midnight oil solely for them.

Civil Service Grade

With a civil service job in your background, you will have been awarded a civil service grade. So, in looking for a job with the government, be sure to list it. In transferring from the government to the private sector, you are best advised to translate it into generic terms and ignore the grade altogether, unless you are applying for jobs with government contractors, subcontractors, or other specialized employers familiar with the intricacies of civil service ranking.

Publications and Patents

Such achievements, if they appear, are usually found at the end of the best resumes. Although they serve as positive means of evaluation for the reader, these achievements are of relatively minor importance in many professions.

Nevertheless, both publications and patents are manifestations of original thought and extended effort above and beyond the call of accepted professionalism. They tell the reader that you invest considerable personal time and effort in your career and are therefore a cut above the competition. Publication carries more weight in some industries and professions (where having literary visibility is synonymous with getting ahead); patents are a definite plus in the technology and manufacturing fields. You will notice in the resume examples how the writers list dates and names of publications, but do not usually include copyright information.

"New Developments in the Treatment of Chronic Pain." 1987. *New England Journal of Medicine.*

"Radical Treatments for Chronic Pain." 1986. *Journal of American Medicine.*

"Pain: Is It Imagined or Real?" 1986. *OMNI Magazine.*

Languages

Technology is rapidly changing our world into the proverbial global village. This means that today, as all companies are interested in client-base expansion, a linguistic edge in the job hunt could be just what you need. If you are fluent in a foreign language, you will want to mention it. Likewise if you understand a foreign language, but perhaps are not fluent, still mention it:

Fluent in French
Read and write Serbo-Croation
Read German
Understand Spanish

Education

Educational history is normally listed whenever it helps your case, although the exact positioning of the information will vary according to the length of your professional experience and the relative strength of your academic achievements.

If you are recently out of school with little practical experience, your educational credentials, which probably constitute your primary asset, will appear near the beginning of the resume.

As you gain experience your academic credentials become less important, and gradually slip toward the end of your resume. The exception to this is found primarily in certain professions where academic qualifications dominate a person's career—medicine, for instance.

You will notice that all examples for education are in reverse chronological order: The highest level of attainment (not necessarily a degree) always comes first, followed by the lesser levels. In this way, a doctorate will be followed by a master's degree, then a bachelor's. For degreed professionals, there is no need to go back further into educational history. (It is optional to list your prestigious prep school.) Those who attended school but did not graduate should nevertheless list the school in its proper chronological position, but should not draw attention to the fact that they did not receive a degree.

Those who did not achieve the higher levels of educational recognition will list their own highest level of attainment. A word on attainment is in order here. If you graduated from high school, attended college, but didn't graduate, you may be tempted to list your high school diploma first, followed by the name of the college you attended. That would give the wrong emphasis: it says you are a college drop-out and focuses on you as high school graduate. In this instance you would in fact list your college and omit reference to earlier educational history.

While abbreviations are frowned on in most circumstances, it is acceptable to abbreviate educational degrees (Ph.D. M.A., A.B, etc), simply because virtually everyone understands them.

Those with scholarships and awards will list them, and recent graduates will usually also list majors and minors (space permitting). The case is a little more confused for the seasoned professional. Many human resources professionals say it makes life easier for them if majors and minors are listed, so they can further sift and grade the applicants. That's good for them, but it might not be good for you. All you want the resume to do is get you in the door, not slam it in your face. So, as omitting these minutiae will never stop you from getting an interview, I strongly urge you to err on the side of safety and leave 'em out.

If you are a recent entrant into the workplace, both your scholastic achievements and your contributions have increased importance. Certainly, you will list your position on the school newspaper or the student council, memberships in clubs, and recognition for scholastic achievement, in short, anything that demonstrates your potential as a productive employee. As your career progresses, however, prospective employers care less and less about your school life and more and more about your work life. If you have five years of work experience and still feel compelled to list your chairmanship of the school's cafeteria committee, then you are not concentrating on the right achievements.

Changing times have also changed thinking about listing fraternities and sororities on resumes. A case could be made, I think, for leaving them off as a matter of course: If such organizations are important to an interviewer he or she will ask. My ruling, however, is that if the resume is tailored to an individual or company, where membership in such organizations will result in a case of "deep calling to deep," then by all means, list. If, on the other hand, the resume is for general distribution, forget it.

Professional Training

Under the educational heading on smart resumes, you will often see a section for continuing professional education, focusing on special courses and seminars attended. Specifically, if you are computer literate, unlike 90% of the country, you will include this strong plus.

Summer and Part-time Employment

This should only be included when the resume writer is either just entering the workforce or re-entering it after a substantial absence. The entry-level person can feel comfortable listing dates and places and times. The returnee should include the skills gained from part-time employment in a fashion that minimizes the "part-time" aspect of the experience; probably by using a Functional resume format.

What Can Never Go In

Some information just doesn't belong in resumes. Make the mistake of including it, and at best your resume loses power. At worst, you fail to land the interview.

Titles: Resume, Fact Sheet, Curriculum Vitae, etc.

Never use any of these variations on a theme as a heading. Their appearance on a resume is redundant: If it isn't completely obvious from the very look of your piece of paper that it is a resume, go back to square one. By the way, there is no difference in meaning between the above terms. "Curriculum Vitae" (or CV, as it is sometimes known) was an early term much favored in English and American academia—basically to prove that the users knew a little Latin. Its use today is outmoded and affected. "Fact Sheet," on the other hand, was a term developed by the employment agencies to imply they were presenting unvarnished facts. The phrase has never caught on.

Availability

Saying anything about your availability for employment on a resume is another redundancy. If you are not available, then why the heck are you wasting everyone's time and slowing down the mails? The only justification for the item's inclusion is if you may expect to be finishing a project and moving on at such and such a time, and not before. But your view should be that intelligent human beings always have their eyes and ears open for better career opportunities—because no one else is going to watch out for them. If leaving before the end of a project could affect your integrity and/or references, O.K. There's a lot to be said for not burning your bridges, and as careers progress, it's surprising how many of the same people you bump into again and again.

Let the subject of availability come up at the face-to-face meeting. After meeting you, an employer will often be prepared to wait until you are available, and will probably appreciate your integrity. If, on the other hand, the employer just sees a resume that says you won't be available until next year—well, you'll just never get to a face-to-face meeting in the first place.

Reason for Leaving

There is no real point to stating your reasons for leaving a job on a resume, yet time and again they are included—to the detriment of the writer. The topic is always covered during an interview anyway. Mentioning it in advance and on paper can only damage your chances for being called in for that meeting.

References

It is inappropriate and unprofessional to list the names of references on a resume. You will never see it on a top example. Why? Interviewers are not interested in checking them before they meet and develop a strong interest in you—it's too time-consuming. In addition, employers are forbidden by law to check references without your written consent (thanks to the 1972 Fair Credit and Reporting Act), and they have to meet you first in order to obtain it, right?

Most employers will assume that references are available anyway (and if they aren't available, boy, are you in trouble). For that reason, there's an argument to be made for leaving that famous line—References Available on Request—off the end of the resume. I disagree, however. It may not be absolutely necessary to say that references are there for the asking, but those four extra words certainly don't do any harm and may help you stand out from the crowd. Including the phrase sends a little message: "Hey, look, I got no skeletons in my closet."

A brief but important aside. If you have ever worked under a different surname, you must take this fact into account when giving your references. A recently-divorced woman wasted a strong interview performance not too long ago because she was using her maiden name on her resume and at the interview. She forgot to tell the employer that her references would, of course, remember her by a different last name. The results of this oversight were catastrophic. Three prior employers denied ever having heard of anyone by the name the woman's interviewer supplied. She lost the job.

Written Testimonials

Even worse than listing references on a resume is to attach a bunch of written testimonials. It is an absolute no-no. No one believes them anyway.

Of course, that doesn't mean that you shouldn't solicit such references for your files. They can always be produced when references are requested and can be used as a basis for those third-party endorsements we talked about. This will be especially helpful to you if you are just entering the work-force, or re-entering after a long absence, because the content of the testimonials you get can be used to beef up your resume significantly.

Salary

Leave out all references to salary, past and present—it is far too risky. Too high or too low a salary can knock you out of the running even before you hear the starting gun. Even in responding to a help-wanted advertisement that specifically requests salary requirements, don't give them. A good resume will still get you the interview, and in the course of your discussions with the company, you'll certainly talk about salary anyway. If you somehow feel obliged to give salary requirements, simply write "competitive" or "negotiable" (and then only in your cover letter).

Abbreviations

With the exceptions of educational attainments, and those required by the postal service, avoid abbreviations if possible at all. Of course, space constraints might make it imperative that you write "No. Wilshire Blvd." instead of "North Wilshire Boulevard." If that is the case, be sure to be consistent. If you abbreviate in one address, abbreviate in all of them. But bear in mind that you will always seem more thoughtful and professional if everything is spelled out. And anyway, your resume will be easier to read!

Jargon

A similar warning applies to industry slang. Your future boss might understand it, but you can bet your boots that neither his or her boss nor the initial resume screener will. Your resume must speak clearly of your skills to many different people, and one skill that we all need today is a sensitivity to the needs of communication.

If you are in one of the high technology industries, however, avoiding jargon and acronyms is not only impossible, it is often inadvisable. All the same, keep the non-technical resume screener in mind before you wax lyrical about bits and bytes.

Charts and Graphs

Even if charts and graphs are part of your job, they make poor use of the space available on a resume—and they don't help the reader. In fact, you should never even bring them out at an interview unless requested. The same goes for other examples of your work. If you are a copywriter or graphic artist, for example, it is all right to say that samples are available, but only if you have plenty of resume space to spare.

Mention of Age, Race, Religion, Sex, National Origin

Government legislation was enacted some years ago forbidding employment discrimination in these areas. So, if the government had to take action, you know things were bad. Although today it's much better, I urge you to leave out any reference to any of these areas in your resume.

Photographs

In days of old, when men were bold and all our cars had fins, it was the done thing to have a photograph in the top right-hand corner of the resume. So, if you are looking for a job in the 1950's, include one; if not, don't. Today, the fashion is against photographs; including them is a waste of space that says nothing about your ability to do a job.

(Obviously, careers in modeling, acting, and certain aspects of the electronic media require photos, because, in these instances, your face is your fortune.)

Health/Physical Description

Who cares? You are trying to get hired, not dated. Unless your physical health (gym instructor, e.g.) and/or appearance (model, actor, media personality) are immediately relevant to the job, leave these issues alone.

Early Background

I regularly see resumes that tell about early childhood and upbringing. To date, the most generous excuse I can come up with for such anecdotes is that the resumes were prepared by the subjects' mothers.

Weaknesses

Any weakness, lack of qualifications, or information likely to be detrimental to your cause should always be canned. Never tell resume readers what you don't have or what you can't or haven't had the opportunity to do yet. Let them find that out for themselves.

Demands

You will never see demands on a good resume. Don't outline what you feel an employer is expected to give or to provide. The time for making demands is when the employer has demonstrated sincere interest in you by extending a job offer with a salary and job description attached. That is when the employer will be interested and prepared to listen to what you want. Until then, concentrate on bringing events to that happy circumstance by emphasizing what you can bring to the employer. In your resume you should, to paraphrase the great man, ask not what your employer can do for you, but rather what you can do for your employer.

Exaggerations

Avoid verifiable exaggerations of your skills, accomplishments, and educational qualifications. Research has now proven that three out of every ten resumes feature inflated educational qualifications. Consequently, verification, especially of educational claims, is on the increase. If you were discovered to have told a sly one on your resume after you had been hired, it could cost you your job and a lot more. The stigma of deceit will very likely follow you for the rest of your professional days. On the other hand, I don't notice 30% of the workforce stumbling around with crippled careers. Matters are tightening up in this area, and ultimately it will be a personal judgment call. Ask yourself, "Do I have a defensible position, should this matter come under scrutiny now or at a later date?"

Judgment Calls

Here are some additional areas that fall neither into the do nor into the don't camp. They are those considerations that will be included depending on your personal circumstances.

Summary

The summary, when it is included in a resume, comes immediately after the Objective. The point is to encapsulate your experience and perhaps highlight one or two of your skills and/or contributions. You hope, in two or three short sentences, to grab the reader's attention with a power pack of the skills and attributes you have developed throughout your career. Good summaries are short; you don't want to show all your aces in the first few lines! (You can see examples of resumes with strong summaries in the resume section of this book.)

On the other hand, many experts feel that the content of the summary must be demonstrated by the body of the resume, and therefore summaries are pointless duplications and a waste of space. The choice is yours. Used wisely and well, they can work.

Personal Flexibility, Relocation

If you are open to relocation for the right opportunity, make it clear. It will never in and of itself get you an interview, but it won't hurt. On the other hand, never state that you aren't open to relocation. After all, that factor usually comes into play only when you have a job offer to consider. Let nothing stand in the way of a nice collection of job offers!

Career Objectives

These are O.K. to include at the very start of your career, before your general direction has been confirmed by experience and track record. Inclusion is also acceptable if you have very clearly defined objectives and are prepared to sacrifice all other opportunities. If that is the case, state your goals clearly and succinctly, remembering not to confuse the nature of long-term career objectives with short-term ones of job objectives.

Beware, though, of the drawbacks. First of all, resume readers aren't famous for paying much attention to objectives. Second, I have seen these used on many occasions to make a hiring decision between two candidates. The resumes are compared, A has no objective, B has an objective that doesn't match the initial expectations. Result? A gets the job. Another consideration is that your resume may be on file for years, during which time your objectives are bound to change. You don't need last year's dusty dreams clouding over your bright tomorrows.

Marital Status

If you think mention of your marital status will enhance your chances (if you are looking for a position as a long distance trucker, marriage counselor, or traveling salesperson, for example) include it. In all other instances leave it out. Legally, your marital status is of no consequence.

Military

Include your good military record with highest rank, especially if you are applying for jobs in the defense sector. Otherwise exclude it: It is no longer any detriment to your career not to have a military history.

Personal Interests

A recent Korn Ferry study showed that executives with team sports on their resumes were seen to be averaging $3000 a year more than their more sedentary counterparts. Now, that makes giving a line to your hobbies worthwhile, if they fit into certain broad categories. These would include team sports (baseball, basketball), determination activities (running, swimming, climbing, bicycling), and "brain actvivities" (bridge, chess).

The rule of thumb, as always, is only to include activities that can in some way contribute to your chances. If you can draw a valid connection, include them; if not, don't.

Personal Paragraphs

Here and there throughout the resume section of this book you will see resumes that include—often toward the end—a short personal paragraph that gives you a candid snapshot of the resume writer as a person. Done well, these can be exciting, effective endings to a resume, but they are not to everyone's taste. Typically, they refer to one or two personal traits, activities, and sometimes, beliefs. These are often tied in with skills required for the particular job sought.

The idea is to make the reader say, "Hey, there's a real person behind those Foster Grants, let's get him in here; sounds like our kind of guy." Of course, as no one can be all things to all people, you won't want to go overboard in this area.

Chapter Four: Resumes That Knock 'em Dead

It has all been theory up to now; this is where the rubber hits the road.

You have a sound idea of why you need a resume; you've had an overview of the different types available to you; and you know what belongs in a powerful resume and what doesn't. We now move from the abstract to the intensely practical side of resume writing.

This is the part of the book that requires you to do some thinking; I will ask questions to jog your memory about your practical experience. The outcome will be a smorgasbord of your most sellable professional attributes. The work we do together in this chapter will not only form the foundation of your resume, but will also prepare you to turn those job interviews into job offers.

People change jobs for a multitude of reasons. Perhaps your career isn't progressing as you want it. Perhaps you have gone as far as you can with your present employer, and the only way to take another career step is to change companies. Maybe you have been in the same job for three or more years, without dramatic salary increases or promotions, and you know that you are going nowhere. You have been stereotyped, classified, and pigeonholed.

Whether you are a fast-tracker, recent graduate, workforce re-entrant, career changer, or what have you, if you are considering new horizons, you must take stock before stepping out.

You need to know where you've been, where you are, and where you're headed. Without this stock-taking, the chances of reaching your ultimate goals are reduced, because you won't know how best to use what you've got to get what you want.

Believe it or not, very few people have a clear fix on what they do for a living. Oh, I know; you ask a typist what he or she does, and you get, "Type, stupid." You ask an accountant, and you hear, "Fiddle with numbers, what do you think?" And that is the problem. Most people don't look at their work beyond these simplistic terms. They never examine the implications of their jobs in relation to the overall success of the department and company. Most people miss not only their importance to an employer as part of the business, but also, their importance to themselves. Preparing your resume will give you a fresh and more lucid view of yourself as a professional and your role in your chosen profession.

Employers all want to know the same thing: How can you contribute to keeping their ship afloat and seaworthy? No one is hired merely to be a typist or an accountant—or anything else, for that matter. Companies hire only one type of person—a problem solver. Look at your work in terms of the problems you solve in the daily round, the problems that would occur if you weren't there.

Some people find the prospect of taking stock of their skills to be an ominous one.

They feel it means judging yourself by others' standards, by the job title and salary assigned to you by someone else. Then, knowing our weaknesses too well, we look at other people in our position, of whom we see only the exterior, and we are awed by their seemingly superior competence, skills, and professionalism. "Seemingly" is the key word here. You are as good as the next person, and to prove it, all you have to do is look yourself squarely in the eye and learn that you have a great deal more to offer than you may ever have imagined. You have solved problems. That's what this chapter is all about.

The Secret of Resume Writing

As a resume writer, you have a lot in common with journalists and novelists. Beginners in each field usually bring some basic misconceptions about how writing is done: I always thought that Stephen King or James Clavell sat down, wrote "Page 1," then three weeks later wrote "The End," and placidly returned the quill to the inkwell. In fact, many professional writers—and resume-writers—have more in common with sculptors. What they really do to start the creative process is to write masses of notes. This great mass is the raw material, like a block of stone, at which you chip away to reveal the masterwork that has been hiding there all along.

The key is that the more notes you have, the better. Just remember that whatever you write in the note-making part of your resume preparation will never suffer public scrutiny. It is for your private consumption; from these notes, the finished work of art will emerge for public view.

This chapter is going to help you write those notes, as you recapture all those forgotten moments of glory that employers love to hear about.

The only difficult step to take is the first one. So pick up a pen and some paper, and plunge ahead right now, without even pausing for breath.

Questionnaire, Part One: Raw Materials

This questionnaire is set up to follow your entire career. In answering the questions as completely as you can, you are creating the mass of raw material from which you will sculpt the final work of art.

1. Current or Last Employer: This includes part-time or voluntary employment if you are a recent graduate or about to re-enter the work-force after an absence. Try looking at your school as an employer and see what new information you reveal about yourself.

> Starting Date:
> Starting Salary:
> Leaving Date:
> Leaving Salary:

2. Company Description: Write one sentence that describes the product(s) your company made or the service(s) it performed.

3. Title: Write your starting job title (the one given to you when you first signed on with the company). Then write a one- or two-sentence description of your responsibilities in that position.

4. Duties: What were your three major duties in this position?

5: Methods, Skills, Results: Now, for each of the above three duties, answer the following questions:

What special skills or knowledge did you need to perform this task satisfactorily?

What has been your biggest achievement in this area? (Try to think about money saved or made, or time saved for the employer. Don't worry if your contributions haven't been acknowledged in writing and signed in triplicate, as long as you know them to be true without exaggeration.)

What verbal or written commments were made about your contributions in this area, by peers or managers?

What different levels of people did you have to interact with to achieve your job tasks? How did you get the best out of Superiors? Co-workers? Subordinates?

What aspects of your personality were brought into play when executing this duty? (For example, perhaps it required attention to detail, or determination, or good verbal and writing skills. Whatever, jot them all down.)

To help you address that last issue (it's a vitally important one), you should look over the following list of a number of personality traits that are in constant demand from all employers.

Analytical Skills: Weighing the pros and cons. Not jumping at the first solution to a problem that presents itself.

Chemistry: Your willingness to get along with others and get the job done.

Communication Skills: More than ever, the ability to talk with and write effectively to people at all levels in a company is a key to success.

Confidence: Poised, friendly, honesty and openness with all employees—high and low.

Dedication: Doing whatever it takes to get the job done.

Drive & Determination: A desire to get things done. Goal oriented. Someone who does not back off when a problem or situation gets tough.

Economy: Most problems have an expensive solution and one that the company would prefer to implement.

Efficiency: Always keeping an eye open for inefficient uses of time, effort, resources and money.

Energy: Extra effort in all aspects of the job, the little things as well as the important matters.

Honesty/Integrity: Responsibility for all your actions—both good and bad. Always making decisions in the best interests of the company, rather than on whim or personal preference.

Listening Skills: Listening, rather than just waiting your turn to speak.

Motivation: Enthusiasm, finding reasons to accept challenges rather than avoid them. A company realizes a motivated person accepts added challenges and does that little bit extra on every job.

Pride: Pride in a job well done. Paying attention to detail.

Reliability: Follow through, a willingness to keep management informed, and a predisposition toward relying on oneself—not others—to see your job done.

Sensitivity to Procedures: Following the chain of command, recognizing that procedures exist to keep a company functioning and profitable. Those who rush to implement their own "improved procedures" wholesale, or organize others to do so, can cause untold chaos in an organization.

6. Supporting Points: If you asked for a promotion or a raise while in this position, what arguments did you use to back up your request?

7. Most Recent Position: Write down your current (or last) job title. Then write a one- or two-sentence description of your responsibilities in that position, and repeat steps three through six. In this step, it is assumed that you have a title and responsibilities that are different from those you had when you first joined the company. If this is not the case, simply ignore this step. On the other hand, many people have held three or four titles with a specific employer, and gained breadth of experience with each one. In this instance, for each different intermediary title, repeat steps one through six. The description of responsibilities should be reserved for your departing (or current) title.

8. Reflecting on Success: Make some general observations about work with this employer. Looking back over your time with this employer, what was the biggest work-related problem that you had to face? What solution did you find? What was the result of the solution when implemented? What was the value to the employer in terms of money earned or saved and improved efficiency? What was the area of your greatest personal improvement in this job? What was the greatest contribution you made as a team player? Who are the references you would hope to use from this employer, and what do you think they would say about you?

9. Getting All the Facts: Repeat the last eight steps for your previous employer, and then for the employer before that, and so forth. Most finished resumes focus on the last three jobs, or last ten years of experience (whichever comes first). In this developmental portion of the process, however, you must go back in time and cover your entire career. Remember that you are doing more than preparing a resume here: You are preparing for the heat of battle in the interview, when all the tough questions start flying. In your initial interview preparation, throughout any telephone screening interviews, and especially before that crucial face-to-face meeting, you can use this Questionnaire to prepare yourself for anything the interviewer might ask. One of the biggest complaints interviewers have about job candidates, and one of the major reasons for rejection, is unpreparedness: "You know, good as some of this fellow's skills are, something just wasn't right. He seemed—slow somehow. You know, he couldn't even remember when he joined his current employer!" You won't have that problem.

Questionnaire, Part Two: Details, Details, Details

The hard work is done and it's all downhill from here. Just fill in the facts and figures relating to the following questions. Obviously, not everything will apply to you. The key is just to put it all down; you can polish it later.

Military History

Include branch of service, rank, and any special skills that could further your civilian career.

Educational History

Start with highest level of attainment and work backwards. Give dates, schools, majors, minors, grade-point averages.

Specify any scholarships or other special awards.

List other school activities, such as sports, societies, social activities. Especially important are leadership roles: Any example of how you "made a difference" with your presence could be of value to your future. Obviously, this is important for recent graduates with little work experience.

Languages

Specify fluency and ability to read and write foreign languages.

Personal Interests

List interests and activities that could be supportive to your candidacy. For example, an internal auditor who plays chess or bridge would list these and probably use them in a resume, because they support the analytical bent so necessary to the work.

Computer Literacy

If you are computer literate, let's have the details. (If not, maybe it's time to wake up and smell the coffee: A knowledge of computers could be critical to your professional survival.)

Patents

Include patents that are both pending and awarded.

Publications

If you have published articles, list the name of the publication, title of article and the publication date. If you have had books published, list the title and publisher.

Professional Associations

Include membership and the details of any offices you held.

Volunteer Work

Also include any volunteer work you performed. It isn't only paid work experience that makes you valuable.

Miscellaneous Areas of Achievement

All professions and careers are different. Use this section to itemize any additional aspects of your history where you somehow "made a difference" with your presence.

Questionnaire, Part Three: Where Are You Going?

Knowing where you want to go will determine both the wording and the layout of your resume. There is an old saying that if you don't know where you are going, you have no hope of getting there. Remember that there is a difference between valid objectives and pipedreams. Dreams aren't bad things to have, but they mustn't be confused with making a living.

Your first step is to write down a job title that embraces your objectives. Having taken this simple step, you need to note underneath it all the skills and qualifications needed to do that job successfully. List them like this:

Job Title

1. First skill
2. Second skill
3. Third skill
4. Fourth skill
5. Fifth skill

But remember that your thoughts on what it takes may not jibe with the employer's thoughts. And what if you are simply not sure what it takes to do the job at all? Simple. Take a trip to the library and ask to see a copy of the *Dictionary of Occupational Titles*. It gives you endless job titles, as you might expect, and brief job descriptions. Make notes by all means, but don't copy it out word for word. The book is full of dead prose that's copper-bottom guaranteed to send the average resume-reader to sleep in three seconds flat. You want to avoid letting any of this soporific stuff sneak into the final draft of your resume.

When you have decided on an objective, and defined what it takes to do that job, go back through the first part of the questionnaire and flag all the entries you can use to build a viable resume. Just underline or highlight the appropriate passages for further attention when the time comes for putting pen to paper.

The chances are that you will find adequate skills in your background to qualify you for the job objective. And, remember: Few people have all the qualifications for the jobs they get!

If you still aren't sure, develop a "Matching Sheet" for yourself. List the practical requirements of your job objective on one side of a piece of paper and match them on the other side with your qualifications. A senior computer programmer, looking for a step up to a systems analysis position with a new job in financial applications, might develop a Matching Sheet that looks like this:

Job Needs	My Experience
Mainframe IBM experience	6 yrs. experience
IBM COBOL	COBOL, PL/1, Assembler
Financial experience	6 yrs. in banking
Sys. dev. methodology	Major sys. dev., 3 yrs.
Communication	Ongoing customer service work OS/MVS, TSO/SPF, CICS, SNAOS/MVS, TSO/SPF, ROSCOE, IMS, DB/DC, SAS

But what about the junior accountant who had VP of finance as a goal? Naturally, at this stage, many of the needed skills—and much of the experience—aren't in place. If you fall into this category, don't worry. You just happened upon a career objective rather than a job objective. To solve the dilemma, list all the title changes between your present position and dream job. This will show you how many career steps stand between you and your ultimate goal. Your job objective is simply the title above your own, the first achievable stepping stone toward the ultimate goal.

At best, job and career objectives are simply a tool to give you focus for writing the resume, and to give the reader something to take sightings on. The way the world is changing, by the time you can reasonably expect to reach your ultimate career goal, that particular position may not even exist.

Be content with a generalized objective for the next job. And don't be afraid of that objective—you aren't taking holy orders, you're identifying a job you'd like to win. Who knows what the next few years will hold for you?

(**Note:** You will find an example of a completed questionnaire on page 211. You'll also find examples of chronological, functional, and combination resumes based on the completed questionnaire on pages 73-77.)

Chapter Five: Writing the Basic Resume

Advertisements and resumes have a great deal in common.

You will notice that the vast majority of advertisements in any media can be heard, watched, or read in under thirty seconds. That is not accidental. The timing is based on studies relating to the limit of the average consumer's attention span.

And that is why you sometimes notice that both resumes and advertisements depart from the rules that govern all other forms of writing. First and last they are an urgent business communication, and business likes to get to the point.

Before putting pen to paper, good advertising copywriters imagine themselves in the position of their target audience. They imagine their objective—selling something. Then they consider what features their product possesses and what benefits it can provide to the purchaser.

You will find a similar procedure beneficial in your own writing. Fortunately, your approach is simplified somewhat, because you can make certain generalizations. You can assume, for instance, that the potential employer has a position to fill and a problem to solve, and that he or she will hire someone who is able to do the job, who is willing to do it, and who is manageable.

For the next fifteen minutes, imagine yourself in one of your target companies. You are in the personnel department, on resume detail. Fortunately, it is a slow morning, and there are only thirty that need to be read. Go straight to the example section now and read thirty resumes without a break, then return to this page.

Now you have some idea of what it feels like. Except that you had it easy—the resumes you read were good, interesting ones, resumes that got real people real jobs. Even so, you probably felt a little punch drunk at the end of the exercise. But I know that you learned a very valuable lesson: Brevity is to be desired above all other things.

Preparation

There is nothing worse than sitting down with the old quill pen, ready to create words of deathless prose, only to discover you forgot the parchment. Getting everything you'll need together first will help you beat that other enemy of the muse—procrastination. Collect:

- A pad of 8½″ × 11″ paper

- Pens, pencils, a computer or typewriter—whatever is your chosen method of writing

- A dictionary. Even your kids' dictionary is O.K. (At least it will restrain you from using those confusing 19-cent words.)

- An old resume, some generic job descriptions, and, of course the completed Questionnaire.

- A ruler—it's useful for keeping things aligned as you lay out and write your resume.

Now, just write. Don't even try for style or literacy—you can tend to that later. Think of yourself as speaking on paper. You'll find your personal speech rhythms will make for a lively resume, once they have been edited.

Choose a Layout

You have seen the basic examples of chronological, functional, and combination resumes in Chapter Two, and certainly you have browsed through the dozens of actual resumes. Find one that strikes your fancy and fits your needs, and use it as your model. It need not reflect your field of professional expertise. Obviously, you will have to tinker with any model, adding or deleting jobs and making other subtle adjustments as necessary, to fashion it for your background.

The first step is just like painting by numbers. Go through the model and fill in the obvious slots—name, address, telephone number(s), employer names, employment dates, educational background and dates, extramural activities and the like. Shazam! Now the first half of your resume is complete.

Filling in the Picture: Chronological Resumes
Objectives

You can have a simple non-specific objective, one that gives the reader a general focus, such as, "Objective: Data Processing Management." It gets the message across succinctly; and if there is no immediate need for someone of your background, it encourages the employer to put your resume in the file where you feel it belongs. That's important, because even if you are not suitable for today's needs, there's a good chance that the resume will be pulled out when such a need does arise.

If you choose to use an expanded, detailed objective, refer to Chapter Three. You will of course:

- Keep it short, just one to two sentences.

- Express your objective in the fewest possible words that can bring a picture to the reader's mind.

- Not get too specific—no one is that interested.

- Focus the objective on what you can do for the company and avoid mention of what you want in return.

- State exactly the job title you seek, if the resume is in response to a specific advertisement.

- Keep your objective general to give yourself the widest number of employment options, if the resume will be sent out "blind" to a number of companies.

Of course with your resume either written or produced on a computer, your objective can go through subtle variations for each specific job.

If you want to use both a non-specific and a detailed objective, headline the resume with the nonspecific title, and then follow with the more detailed one.

Company Role

Now, for each employer, edit your response from step two of the Questionnaire, which outlines that company's services or products. Make it one short sentence: Do not exceed one line or ten words.

Job Titles

Remember what we said in Chapter Three. There is nothing intrinsically wrong with listing your title as "Fourth-level Administration Clerk, Third Class," as long as you are prepared to wait until doomsday for it to be considered by someone who understands what it means and is able to relate it to current needs. With this in mind:

- Be general in your job title. All companies have their particular ways of dispensing job titles, and they all vary. Your title with employer A will mean something entirely different to employer B, and might not make any sense at all to employer C.

- Whenever possible, stay away from designations such as trainee, junior, intermediate, senior—as in Junior Engineer—and just designate yourself as Engineer, Designer, Editor, or what have you.

Responsibilities

In a chronological resume, the job title is often followed by a short sentence that helps the reader visualize you doing the job. Get the information from the completed questionnaire and do a rough edit to get it down to one short sentence. Don't worry about perfection now; the polishing is done later.

The responsibilities and contributions you list here are those functions that best display your achievements and problem-solving abilities. They do not necessarily correspond with how you spent the majority of your working day, nor are they related to how you might prefer to spend your working day. Problems sometimes arise by mistakenly following either of these paths. It can perhaps best be illustrated by showing you part of a resume that came to my desk recently. It is the work of a professional who listed her title and duties for one job like this:

> Sales Manager: Reponsible for writing branch policy, coordination of advertising and advertising agencies. Developed knowledge of IBM PC. Managed staff of six.

Is it any wonder she wasn't getting responses to her resume-mailing campaign? Here, she has explained where she was spending her time when the resume was created. The explanation, however, has nothing to do with the major functions of her job. She has mistakenly listed everything in the reverse chronological order, not in relation to the items' relative importance to a future employer. Let's look at what subsequent restructuring achieved:

> Sales Manager: Hired to turn around stagnant sales force. Successfully recruited, trained, managed and motivated a consulting staff of six. Result: 22% sales gain over first year.

In the re-write of this particular part of the resume, notice how she thought like a copywriter and quickly identified the problem she was hired to solve.

> Hired to turn around stagnant sales force. (Demonstrates her skills and responsibilities.)

> Successfully recruited, trained, managed and motivated a consulting staff of six. Result: 22% sales gain over first year. (Shows what she subsequently did about them, and just how well she did it.)

By doing this, her responsibilities and achievements become more important in the light of the problems they solved.

Some More About Contributions

Business has very limited interests. In fact, those interests can be reduced to a single sentence: Making a profit. Making a profit is done in just three ways: By saving money in some fashion for the company; by saving time through some innovation at the company, which in turn saves the company money and gives it the opportunity to make more money in the time saved; or by simply making money for the company.

That's all there is to any business when you reduce things to their simplest forms.

That does not mean that you should address only those points in your resume and ignore valuable contributions which cannot be quantified. But it does mean that you should try to quantify as much as you can.

If you find it difficult to recall and prioritize your responsibilities at a given company, go to the library and consult the *Directory of Job Descriptions.* But, as I have said before, be careful. If you do resort to this as a memory jogger be careful not to copy out the appropriate entry in its entirety — the prose is deadly boring.

Achievements

Your achievements will be listed in step five of the first part of the Questionnaire. The achievements you take from step five will not necessarily be the greatest things you have accomplished on planet Earth, but they will be the greatest accomplishments that can help you reach your stated (or unstated) employment objective. Concentrate solely on those topics that relate to your objectives, even if it means leaving out some significant achievement; you can always rectify the situation at the interview.

Pick two to four accomplishments for each job title and edit them down to bite-size chunks that read like a telegram. Write as if you had to pay for each entry by the word—this approach can help you pack a lot of information into a short space. The resulting abbreviated style will help convey a sense of immediacy to the reader.

> Responsible for new and used car sales. Earned "Salesman of the Year" awards, 1985 and 1986. Record holder for:
>
> • Most Cars Sold in One Month

- Most Cars Sold in One Year

- Most Board Gross in One Month

- Most Board Gross in One Year

- Created an annual giving program to raise operating funds. *Raised $2,000,000.*

- Targeted, cultivated, and solicited sources including individuals, corporations, foundations, state and federal agencies. *Raised $1,650,000.*

- Raised funds for development of the Performing Arts School facility, capital expense, and music and dance programs. *Raised $6,356,000.*

Now, while you may tell the reader about these achievements, you should never explain how they were accomplished. After all, the idea of the resume is to pique interest and to raise as many questions as you answer. Questions mean interest, and getting that interest satisfied requires talking to you!

You probably have lots of great accomplishments to share with the reader that will tempt you to add a second page, or even a third. Your resume, however, is designed to form the basis for tantalizing further discussions, so just be content with showing the reader a little glimpse of the gold vein—and let him or her discover the rest of the strike later. Very often, the information discovered by the interviewer's own efforts takes on greater value than information offered free of charge on paper. Also, you have saved some of your heavy firepower for the interview, so that the meeting will not be an anti-climax for the interviewer. And that, in turn, will lend you some leverage and control in the discussions.

Prioritize the listing of your accomplishments as they relate to your job objective, and be sure to quantify your contributions (that is, put them into tangible, profit-oriented terms) wherever possible and appropriate.

Now is the time to weave in one or two of those laudatory quotes (also from step five). Don't include every one, but do incorporate enough to show that others think well of you.

- Sales volume increased from $90 million to $175 million. *Acknowledged as "the greatest single sales gain of the year."*

- Earnings increased from $9 million to $18 million. Review stated, *"always a view for the company bottom line."*

- Three key stores were each developed into $30 million units. Praised for *"an ability to keep all the balls in the air, all the time."*

Functional or Combination Resumes

These resumes are similar to chronological ones in content; often it's just the order of information that is different. Employers and employment dates are downplayed by relegating them to the end of paragraphs, or to the bottom of the resume. Job titles and job responsibilities for specific jobs are sometimes omitted altogether.

In a functional or combination resume, you will have identified the skills and attributes necessary to fulfill the functions of the job objective, and will highlight the appropriate attributes you have to offer. In this format, you will have headings that apply to the skill areas your chosen career path demands, such as: Management, Training, Sales, etc. Each will be followed by a short paragraph packed with selling points. These can be real paragraphs, or the introductory sentence followed by the bullets usually recommended for the chronological formats. Here are examples of each style.

COLLECTIONS:

Developed excellent rapport with customers while significantly shortening pay-out terms *through application of problem-solving techniques.* Turned impending loss into profit. Personally salvaged and increased sales with two multi-million dollar accounts by providing remedial action for their sales/financial problems.

COLLECTIONS:

Developed excellent rapport with customers while significantly shortening pay-out terms:

- Evaluated sales performance, offered suggestions for financing/merchandising.

- Performed on-the-spot negotiations; turned impending loss into profit.

- Salvaged two multi-million-dollar problem accounts by providing remedial action for their sales/financial problems. Subsequently increased sales.

Keep each paragraph to an absolute maximum of four lines. This ensures that the finished product has plenty of white space so that it is easy on the reader's eye.

Editing and Polishing

Sentences gain power with verbs that demonstrate an action. For example, one client—a mature lady with ten years at the same law firm in a clerical position—had written in her original resume:

I learned to use a Wang 220VS.

After discussion of the circumstances that surrounded learning how to use the Wang 220VS, certain exciting facts emerged. By using action verbs and an awareness of employer interests, this sentence was charged up, given more punch. Not only that, for the first time the writer fully understood the value of her contributions, which greatly enhanced her self-image:

I analyzed and determined need for automation of an established law office. Responsible for hardware and software selection, installation and loading. Within one year, I had achieved a fully automated office.

Notice how the verbs show that things happen when you are around the office. These action verbs and phrases add an air of direction, efficiency and accomplishment to every resume. They succinctly tell the reader what you did and how well you did it.

Now look at the above example when a third-party endorsement is added to it:

I analyzed and determined need for automation of an established law office. Responsible for hardware and software selection, installation and loading. Within one year, I had achieved a fully automated office. Partner stated, "You brought us out of the dark ages into the technological age, and in the process neither you nor the firm missed a beat!"

Action Verbs

Here are over 180 action verbs and phrases that will be useful to you. Go through the list and see which ones you can use to give punch to your resume writing.

accomplished	engineered	programmed
achieved	enlisted	projected
acted	established	promoted
adapted	evaluated	provided
addressed	examined	publicized
administered	executed	published
advanced	expanded	purchased
advised	expedited	recommended
allocated	explained	reconciled
analyzed	extracted	recorded
appraised	fabricated	recruited
approved	facilitated	reduced
arranged	familiarized	referred
assembled	fashioned	regulated
assigned	focused	rehabilitated
assisted	forecast	remodeled
attained	formulated	repaired
audited	founded	represented
authored	generated	researched
automated	guided	restored
balanced	headed up	restructured
budgeted	identified	retrieved
built	illustrated	reversed
calculated	implemented	reviewed
catalogued	improved	revitalized
chaired	increased	saved
clarified	indoctrinated	scheduled
classified	influenced	schooled
coached	informed	screened
collected	initiated	set
compiled	innovated	shaped
completed	inspected	skilled
composed	installed	solidified
computed	instituted	solved
conceptualized	instructed	specified
conducted	integrated	stimulated
consolidated	intepreted	streamlined
contained	interviewed	strengthened
contracted	introduced	summarized
contributed	invented	supervised
controlled	investigated	surveyed
coordinated	launched	systemized
corresponded	lectured	tabulated
counseled	led	taught
created	maintained	trained
critiqued	managed	translated
cut	marketed	traveled
decreased	mediated	trimmed
delegated	moderated	upgraded
demonstrated	monitored	validated
designed	motivated	worked
directed	negotiated	wrote
developed	operated	
devised	organized	
diagnosed	originated	
directed	overhauled	
dispatched	oversaw	
distinguished	performed	
diversified	persuaded	
drafted	planned	
edited	prepared	
educated	presented	
eliminated	prioritized	
enabled	processed	
encouraged	produced	

Use these words to edit and polish your work, to communicate, persuade and motivate the reader to take action.

This stage is most challenging because many people in different companies will see and evaluate your resume. Keep industry "jargon" to a minimum; there will be some who understand the intricacies and technicalities of your profession, and some who don't. And you need to share your technical or specialist wisdom with the non-specialists, too.

Varying Sentence Structure

Most good writers are at their best writing short punchy sentences. Keep your sentences under about twenty words; a good average is around fifteen. If your sentence is longer than the twenty mark, either shorten it by restructuring, or make two sentences out of the one. The reader on the receiving end has neither the time nor the inclination to read your sentences twice to get a clear understanding.

At the same time, you don't want the writing to sound choppy, so vary the length of sentences when you can. You can also start with a short phrase and follow with a colon:

- Followed by bullets of information;

- Each one supporting the original phrase.

All these different techniques are designed to enliven the reading process. Here's an example of how the above suggestions might be put into practice:

Analyzed and determined need for automation of an established law office:

- Responsible for hardware and software selection;

- Coordinated installation of Wang 220VS and 6 work stations;

- Operated and maintained equipment, and trained other users;

- Full automation achieved in one year.

Partner stated, "You brought us out of the dark ages and neither you nor the firm missed a beat!"

Just as you use short sentences, use common words. They communicate quickly and are easy to understand. Stick to short and simple words wherever possible without sounding infantile. Of course, you need action words and phrases. But the real point is to stay away from obscure words.

Short words for short sentences
help make gripping short paragraphs:
Good for short attention spans!

Within your short paragraphs and short sentences, beware of name and acronym dropping, such as "Worked for Dr. A. Witherspoon in Sys. Gen. SNA 2.31." This is a good way to confuse (and lose) readers. Their coinage is too restricted to have validity outside the small circle of specialists to whom they speak. Your resume deserves the widest possible readership. Apart from the section on the resume that includes your educational qualifications, stay away from jargon unless you work in a highly technical field.

Voice and Tense

The voice you develop for your resume depends on a few important factors: getting a lot said in a small space; being factual; and packaging yourself in the best way.

The voice you use should be consistent throughout the resume. There is considerable disagreement among the experts about the best voice, and each of the leading options have both champions and detractors.

Sentences can be truncated (up to a point) by omitting pronouns—I, you, he, she, it, they, a or the. In fact, many authorities recommend the dropping of pronouns as a technique that both saves space and allows you to brag about yourself without seeming boastful. It gives the impression that another party is writing about you. Many people feel that to use the personal pronoun ("I automated the office") is naive and unprofessional. These experts suggest you use either the third person ("He automated the office") or leave the pronoun out altogether ("Automated office").

At the same time, there are others who recommend that you write in the first person because it makes you sound more human. Use whatever style works best for you. If you do use the personal pronoun, though, try not to use it in every sentence—it gets a little monotonous and takes up valuable space on the page.

A nice variation I have seen is a third-person voice used throughout the resume and then a final few words in the first person appended to the end of the resume, to give an insight into your values. Here is an example:

Regular third person:

James Sharpe is a professional who knows Technical Services from the ground up. He understands its importance in keeping a growing company productive, and takes pride in creating order in the chaos of technology.

Abbreviated third person:

Responsible for machine and system design, production scheduling, procurement scheduling and quality control. Redesigned conveyors and simplified maintenance while improving quality. Instituted a system of material control to account for all materials used.

First person:

I am accustomed to accepting responsibility and delegating authority; and am capable of working with and through people at all levels. Am able to plan, organize, develop, implement and supervise complex programs and special projects. All of this requires a good sense of humor and a personal dedication to producing timely, cost-effective results.

Many people mistake the need for professionalism in a resume with stiff-necked formality. The most effective tone is one that mixes both the conversational and the formal, just the way we do in our offices and on our jobs. The only overriding rule is to make it readable, so that another person can see the human being shining through the pages.

Length

If you are writing in longhand, it can be difficult to judge how your pages of writing will convert to typescript. As a rule of thumb, two and a half pages of double spaced handwriting usually make one page of typescript.

The accepted rules for length are one page for every ten years of your experience. If you have more than twenty years under your belt, however, you won't want to appear to be too steeped in the annals of ancient history and so will not exceed the two-page mark anyway.

Occasionally a three- or four-page resume can be effective, but only in the following two instances:

- You have been contacted directly by an employer about a specific position and have been asked to prepare a resume for that particular opportunity.

- An executive recruiter who is representing you determines that the exigencies of a particular situation warrant an extensive dossier. Usually, such a resume will be prepared exclusively by the recruiter.

You'll find that thinking too much about length considerations while you write will hamper you. Think instead of the story you have to tell, then layer fact upon fact until it is told. When that is done you can go back and ruthlessly cut it to the bone.

Ask yourself these questions:

- Can I cut out any paragraphs?

- Can I cut out any sentences?

- Can I cut out any superfluous words?

- Where have I repeated myself?

If in doubt, cut it out—leave nothing but facts and action words!

And if you find at the end that you've cut out too much, you'll have the additional pleasure of reinstating text!

The Proofreading Checklist for Your Final Draft

There are really two proofing steps in the creation of a polished resume. The first you do at this point, to make sure that all the things that should be in are there—and that all the things that shouldn't, aren't. The final proofing is done after typesetting, and is addressed later in the book.

In the heat of the creative moment, it's easy to miss critical components or mistakenly include facts that give the wrong emphasis. Check your resume against these points:

Contact Information

- Is the pertinent personal data—name, address, and personal telephone number correct? (Later, when the resume is typed or printed, you will want to make sure that this personal data is on every page.)

- Is your business number omitted unless it is absolutely necessary and safe to include it?

Objectives

- Does your objective briefly state your employment goals without getting too specific and ruling you out of consideration for many jobs?

- If you gave a detailed objective (up to—but no more than—two sentences), does it focus on what you can bring to the employer, rather than what you want from the employer?

- Is your stated objective supported by the facts and accomplishments stated in the rest of your resume?

Summary

- If you choose to include a summary, is it no more than two or three sentences long?

- Does it include at least one substantial accomplishment that supports your employment goals?

- Does it include reference to some of your personality or behavioral traits that are critical to success in your field?

Body of Resume

- Is your most relevant and qualifying work experience prioritized throughout the resume to lend strength to your application?

- Have you avoided wasting space with inessential employer names and addresses?

- Have you been suitably discreet with the name of your current employer?

- Have you omitted any reference to reasons for leaving a particular job?

- Have you removed all references to past, current or desired salaries?

- Have you removed references to your date of availability?

Education

- Is education placed in the appropriate position? (It should be at the beginning of the resume if you have little or no work experience; at the end if you are established in your field and your practical experience now outweighs your degree.)

- Is your highest educational attainment shown first?

- Have you included professional courses that support your candidacy?

Chronology

- If you've done a chronological resume, is your work history stated in reverse chronological order, with the most recent employment coming at the head of the resume?

- Within this reverse chronology, does each company history start with details of your most senior position?

- Have you avoided listing irrelevant responsibilities or job titles?

- Does your resume emphasize the contributions, achievements, and problems you have sucessfully solved during your career? Is this content made prominent by underlining, bolding, italicizing, etc.?

- Does the body copy include at least one, and possibly two or three, laudatory, third-party endorsements of your work?

- Have you avoided poor focus by eliminating all extraneous information? (This category includes anything that doesn't relate to your job objective, such as captaining the tiddlywinks team in kindergarten.)

- Have you included any volunteer or community service activities that can lend strength to your candidacy?

- Is the whole thing long enough to whet the reader's appetite for more details, yet short enough not to quench that thirst?

- Have you left out lists of references and only included mention of the availability of references (if, of course, there is nothing more valuable to fill up the space)?

- Have you avoided treating your reader like a fool by highlighting the obvious (i.e., heading your resume, "RESUME")?

Writing Style

- Have you substituted short words for long words? And one word where previously there were two?

- Is your average sentence 10-20 words? Have you made sure that any sentence of more than 20 words is shortened or broken into two sentences?

- Have you kept every paragraph under five lines, with many paragraphs considerably shorter?

- Do your sentences begin, wherever possible, with the powerful action verbs and phrases from earlier in the chapter and from the resume examples?

- If you are in a technical field, have you weeded out as much of the jargon as possible?

Crossing the T's, Dotting the I's

Before you have your resume typed or printed (a topic covered in the next chapter), you have to make sure that your writing is as clear as possible. Three things guaranteed to annoy resume readers are: Incorrect spelling, poor grammar, and improper syntax. Go back and check all these areas. If you feel uneasy about your resume's syntax, you had better get a third party involved.

An acquaintance of mine recently came up with an eminently practical solution to the "style" problem. She went around to the local library, waited for a quiet moment, and got into conversation with the librarian, who subsequently agreed to give her resume the old once-over for spelling, grammar and syntax. You say you're on bad terms with the library because of all those overdue books? Surely you know someone whose opinion you trust in these matters. Enlist him or her. The point is that you must do everything you can to make the resume a "perfect" document before it is typed, printed, or copied.

It simply isn't possible for even the most accomplished professional writer to go directly from final draft to print, so don't try it. Your pride of authorship will blind you to the blemishes, and that's a self-indulgence you can't afford.

You need some distance from your creative efforts to gain detachment and objectivity. There is no hard and fast rule about how long it takes to come up with the finished product. Nevertheless, if you think you have finished, leave it alone as long as you can—at least overnight. Then you can come back to it fresh and read almost as if it were meeting your eyes for the first time.

More Than One Resume?

Do you need more than one type of resume? It depends. Some people have a background that qualifies them for more than one job. If this applies to you, the process is as simple as changing your objective for various employers and rewriting along the lines directed in this chapter.

There is a case for all of us having resumes in more than one format. I was once engaged in an outplacement experiment for a group of professionals. With just a little extra work, we developed chronological, functional, and combination resumes for everyone. The individuals concerned sent out the resume of their choice. Then, in those instances where there was no response, a different version of the resume was sent out. The result from just a different format: eight percent more interviews.

What's Next?

Almost home now. Save your notes, early drafts and, of course, the completed Questionnaire. This "legwork" represents essential material you'll need in updating or revising future versions of your resume.

Chapter Six:
The Final Product

When it comes to clothes, style has a certain look. It has a feel that everyone recognizes but few can define accurately. Fortunately, with resumes, the situation is considerably simplified. There are definite rules to follow.

The Circular File

A lot of resumes get trashed without ever being properly read.

The average resume arrives on a desk along with dozens of others, all of which require screening. Stand in the shoes of a day-in, day-out resume reader, and you can see yourself learning to make some pretty quick decisions. Realistically, you can expect that your resume will get a maximum of 30 to 40 seconds of initial attention. And that's only if it's laid out well and looks clear.

What are the biggest complaints about those resumes that reach the trash can in record time?

Impossible to read. They have too much information crammed into the space and are therefore very difficult to read and hard on the eyes.

Messy. They exhibit amateurish typing.

No coherence. Their layout is unorganized, illogical and uneven. In other words, they look shoddy and slapdash—and who wants an employee like that?

Typos. They are riddled with misspellings.

Here are some tips garnered from the best resumes in America that will help yours rise above the rest.

Typing

Type your own resume only if you are a completely competent typist. What may appear a forgivable little slip to you is simple slovenliness to the reader.

If you can type but don't have a typewriter, your local library will likely have one that you can use. Otherwise, you may wish to try one of the new-style copy shops that rent typewriters and computers by the hour. When renting (or begging or borrowing), be sure you use a professional machine. Many of the so-called "personal typewriters" are incapable of giving you the crisp print necessary to give your resume that "pick-me-up-and-look-at-me" first impression.

Typewriters come in four varieties:

- The old arm-style typewriter. This has fewer features, is outmoded, and is gradually disappearing.

- The ball typewriter, like the standard IBM Selectric, seen in so many offices. It has more technological flexibility than the earlier arm-style type.

- The daisy-wheel typewriter. This uses the same printing apparatus as all but the very latest word processors and computers.

- The new word processing typewriter. A cross between a traditional typewriter and a word processor. These machines only started to hit the market in 1986. They have basic memory capabilities, with editing and layout functions (among other features) and look very promising for the resume writer.

If, like most of us, you aren't a competent typist, pay a professional typist to do the job. Whatever you spend will be more than justified by the appearance of your finished product, and your lowered frustration level. When examining the advertising in your local newspapers and yellow pages, look for those people who advertise a specialty in resumes.

Word Processing Services

The essential difference between using a typewriter and using a word processor is that the word processor has the ability to store information on a disc. That allows spelling and format changes to be made at the touch of a button. Many of the professional free-lance typists now have moved over to word processors. It is distinctly to your advantage to find someone with WP capability. There are two main reasons.

First and foremost, your general resume (the one you can send to anyone) will be stored on a disc. That means that if you want to tailor it for a specific job, on short notice, you can have it done in a matter of minutes. Many of these services will give you such customization at nominal charges. This means that you have the capability of targeting many employers with endless variations of your resume.

In addition, once it's been stored on disc, the resume is ready for updating as long as you live.

In most instances, with word processsing, the printing unit is separate from the computer. Is that important? Yes. Just as all typewriters are not created equal, neither are all printers; and printers are the business end of the machine. They print your resume, and that's the end that a business sees!

When using a word processor—or a word processing service—you must insist that your resume be typed on a letter quality printer or a laser printer; either of these will give you high quality print. You must never accept the type formats known as dot matrix, thermal, or the deceptively-titled near letter quality, often known as NLQ. All these formats lack the razor sharpness you want. *Don't let anyone tell you otherwise.*

A word or two of special advice here. Small companies come and go with great rapidity, so when your resume is finished, ask for three copies of it on disc. Why three? Things happen to discs, as they happen to socks; consequently everyone with any significant computer experience will usually maintain three copies of an important document, each on a separate disc— just to be on the safe side. You might decide to keep two at your home—a working disk and a backup—and the third in a storage facility or, if you have one, a safety deposit box. That way, no matter where you find yourself living next time the old resume needs updating, and no matter what may happen to your primary disc, your resume is available for quick changes.

Ideally, you should get someone with an Apple, Tandy or IBM machine to do your work for you. Computer and software companies also come and go, but these outfits are a good bet to stick around for as long as you're likely to need a resume.

Typesetting

Finally, we address the matter of having your resume professionally typeset. The quality of type appearing in your resume will be of the level found in books, magazines, and newspapers. It is demonstrably superior to that produced by typewriters, and, to a smaller degree, better than text generated from a laser printer.

All the guidelines for choosing typing or word processing services apply to typesetting services. Many typesetting firms have a side specialty in resumes—these are usually an excellent choice.

Your local newspaper may also do resume typesetting as a sideline. They can be expected to charge between $25 and $45.

Typefaces

Some typefaces are easier to read than others. Use, choose or insist on one that is clear and easy on the eye. Avoid fancy script typefaces. Your resume must spell BUSINESS from start to finish.

For ball and daisy-wheel typewriters and printers, the acceptable typefaces are Pica and Elite.

Pica: Now is the time for all good men to come to the aid of their country.

Elite: Now is the time for all good men to come to the aid of their country.

Acceptable typefaces for laser printers, which produce a wide variety of typefaces at very high quality, are Times Roman and Helvetica. These fonts go by various names, and vary slightly from printer to printer. Generally, they look like this:

Times Roman: Now is the time for all good men to come to the aid of their country.

Helvetica: Now is the time for all good men to come to the aid of their country.

Often, you will be able to see the styles available for use before you tell the printer how you want your resume set. Choose the font that most suits your tastes.

How to Brighten the Page

Once you decide on a typeface, stick with it, because more than one on a page looks confusing. You can do plenty to liven up the visual impact of the page within the variations of the typeface you have chosen.

Most typefaces come in a selection of regular, bold, and italics. Good resumes try to take advantage of this—they can vary the impact of key words with italics, underline important phrases, or embolden or capitalize titles for additional emphasis.

You will notice from the examples in this book that the best resumes pick two or three typographical variations and stick with them. For example, a writer who wants to emphasize personality traits might italicize only those words or phrases that describe these aspects. That way the message gets a double fixing in the reader's mind.

Proofing

When you have the typed or typeset resume in hand, you *must* proofread it. Typists are not perfect. Check everything, from beginning to end.

- Is everything set up the way you want it?

- Are there any typographical errors?

- Is all the punctuation correct?

- Has everything been underlined, capitalized, bolded, italicized, and indented, exactly as you specified?

Once you read the resume, try your best to get someone else to review it as well. A third party will always provide more objectivity than you can, and can catch errors you might miss.

Appearance Checklist

- Have you remembered that the first glance and the first feel of your resume can make a powerful impression?

- Have you used only one side of the page?

- If you have employed more than one page for your resume, did you check to make sure that your name, address, and telephone number are on every page?

- If more than one page, did you paginate your resume ("1 of 2" at the bottom of the first page and so on)?

Choosing Your Paper

Quality and care have a look and a feel to them that is loud and clear. Quality paper always makes a favorable impression on the person holding the page.

Beyond the aesthetics, there are plenty of reasons to use quality paper for your copies. The right paper will take the ink better, giving you clean, sharp print resolution.

While you should not skimp on paper cost, neither should you be talked into buying the most expensive available. Indeed, in some fields (healthcare and education come to mind), too ostentatious a paper can cause a negative impression. The idea is to create a feeling of understated quality.

Paper can come in different weights and textures. Good resume-quality paper has a weight designation of between 16 and 25 lbs. Lighter, and you run the risk of appearing nonchalant, unconcerned about the personal "I-printed-this-especially-for-you" aspect of the resume. Heavier, and the paper is unwieldly, like light cardboard.

Paper texture, on the other hand, is a personal decision. You can use a heavy typewriter paper (it is cheaper), but a linen-finished or rag paper will have a more traditional business feel.

As for color, white is considered to be the prime choice. Cream is also acceptable, and I'm assured that some of the pale pastel shades can be both attractive and effective. Personally, I think that most professionals just don't show up in the best light when dressed in pink—call me old-fashioned if you will.

Such pastel shades were originally used to make resumes stand out. But now that everyone is so busy standing out from the crowd in Magenta and Passionate Puce, you might find it more original to stand out in white or cream. Both colors reflect the clean-cut, corporate conservatism of our time. White and cream are straightforward, no-nonsense colors.

Cover letter stationery should always match the color and weight of your resume. To send a white cover letter—even if it is written on your personal stationery—with a cream resume is gauche, and detracts from the powerful statement you are trying to make.

A good idea, in fact, is to print some cover-letter stationery when you produce your finished resume. The letterhead should be in the same typeface and on the same kind of paper, and should copy the contact infomation from your resume. With the advent of word processing, it can take less than five minutes to create the letterhead of your choice.

Copies

Every resume should be printed on standard, 8½" by 11", letter-size paper. If the original is set up like this, you will be able to take it to a good quality copy shop for photocopying. Technology has improved so much in this area that as long as the latest equipment is used, you should have no problems.

If you choose to have your resume printed—rather than photocopied—for whatever reason, you must go to a multi-lith or photo-offset printer. Both produce really smart, professional copies. Of the two—unless you are printing more than 200 copies—photo-offset will be proportionately more expensive. Shop around for prices, as printers vary quite dramatically in their price structures. While you are shopping, ask to see samples of their resume work—they are bound to have some. If not, keep shopping.

Typing and word processing services can not only produce the resume and cover letter stationery, but also the required number of copies of both, as can a multi-lith or offset printer. There are both local and national companies that can provide these services.

The Final Checklist

• Have you used a good-quality paper, with a weight of between 16 and 25 lbs.?

• Does the paper size measure 8½" by 11"?

• Have you used white, off-white, or cream-colored paper?

• If your resume is more than one page, have you stapled the pages together (one staple in the top left-hand corner)?

• Is your cover letter written on stationery that matches your resume?

Chapter Seven
Cover Letters

Do you ever receive junk mail? Of course you do. Who doesn't?

Junk mail. Tons of it have probably made it into your mailbox over the years. Now, what do you do with the stuff marked "Occupant"? Either junk it without reading, or junk it after a quick glance. That's why they call it junk mail! It never gets the attention a personal letter does.

The days when you could dash your resume off to "Personnel", with a clear conscience and no personal note, are long gone. It will be read by the lowest of the low, someone who probably can't even spell "professional." You will be consigning it to the mass resume graveyard that all other impersonally addressed resumes reach.

Your cover letter is the personalizing factor in the presentation of an otherwise essentially impersonal document—your resume. A good cover letter sets the stage for the reader to accept your resume as something special.

So your first effort with a cover letter is to find an individual to whom you can address it. That shows you have focus, and guarantees that a specific individual will open and read it. It also means you have someone to ask for by name when you do your follow-up—important when you are interview hunting.

Your target is someone who can either hire you or refer you to someone who can—and management rather than personnel offers you a much better chance of achieving that goal.

Your cover letter will either be sent to someone as a result of a prior conversation, or sent "cold"—with no prior conversation. You will see how to handle both these eventualities as we progress through the chapter.

When the envelope is opened, your cover letter is the first thing seen. It can make an indelible first impression. I'm not saying that it will get you the job (or even land you the interview), but it will help you along the way by getting that resume read with something akin to serious attention.

The higher up the professional ladder you climb, the more important cover letters become. For the person using written communication in the execution of daily duties (and who doesn't these days?), this letter becomes a valuable vehicle for demonstrating needed job skills.

Cover Letter Rules

Cover letters are brief, never more than a page. Write more, and you will be labeled as an unorganized windbag. You should always try to follow accepted business letter protocol, with the date, employer's name and address first. Space can be at such a premium, however, that you can dispense with the formality and begin with a normal salutation: "Dear _____". Stick with the protocol when you can, ignore it when you have to.

The following four steps will help you create the body of the letter.

Step One

Grab your reader's attention. Do this by using quality stationery. If you don't have personal stationery, use some of the sheets you have bought to have your resume printed on. That way, letter and resume will match and give an impression of balance and continuity. Basic business letters should be laid out according to the accepted standards, like this:

[YOUR ADDRESS/LETTERHEAD
AND TELEPHONE NUMBER]

[DATE]

[ADDRESSEE ADDRESS]

[SALUTATION],

Recently I have been researching the leading local companies in data communications. My search has been for companies that are respected in the field, and who provide on-going training programs. The name of DataLink Products keeps coming up as a top company.

I am an experienced voice and data communications specialist with a substantial background in IBM environments. If you have an opening for someone in this area you will see that my resume demonstrates a person of unusual dedication, efficiency and drive.

My experience and achievements include:

* The complete redesign of a data communications network, projected to increase efficiency company-wide by some 12%.

* The installation and troubleshooting of a Defender II call-back security system for a dial-up network.

I enclose a copy of my resume, and look forward to examining any of the ways you feel my background and skills would benefit DataLink Products. While I prefer not to use my employers time taking personal calls at work, with discretion you can reach me at 213/555-5555 to initiate contact. Let's talk!

Yours,

[SIGNATURE]
[TYPED NAME]

Step Two

Generate interest with the content. You do this by addressing the letter to someone by name, and quickly explaining what you have to offer: The first sentence grabs attention, the rest of the paragraph gives the reader the old one-two punch. The rule is: Say it strong and say it straight; don't pussy-foot around.

A little research, for example, can get your letter off to a fast start.

I came across the enclosed article in Newsweek and thought it might interest you. It encouraged me to do a little research on your company. The research convinced me of two things: You are the kind of people I want to be associated with; and I have the kind of qualifications you can use.

Of course, in the real world, we don't all apply for jobs with companies that are featured in the big magazines. Here are some other examples:

I have been following the performance of your fund in <u>Mutual Funds Newsletter.</u> The record over the last three years shows strong portfolio management. Considering my experience with one of your competitors, I know I could make significant contributions.

Recently I have been researching the local _____ industry. My search has been for companies that are respected in the field and that provide ongoing training programs. The name _____ keeps coming up as a top company.

With the scarcity of qualified and motivated (your desired job title) that exists today, I felt sure that it would be valuable for us to communicate.

I want to be a _____ with your company.

I would like the opportunity to put my _____ years of _____ experience to work for _____.

Within the next few weeks I will be moving from New York to San Francisco. Having researched the companies in my field in my new home town, I know that you are the people I want to talk to.

The state of the art in _____ changes so rapidly that it is tough for most professionals to keep up. I am the exception. I am eager to bring my experience to bear for your company.

I am applying for a position with your company because I know you will find my background and drive interesting.

This letter and the attached resume is in application for employment with _____.

If you are looking for summer jobs:

In six weeks, I shall be finishing my second year at John Carroll University. I am interested in working for your firm during the summer because...

As the summer season gets under way, I know you will be looking for extra help.

I am a high-school senior looking for some real-world experience during the summer break.

I am very interested in becoming one of your summer interns.

If you are writing as the result of a referral, say so and quote the person's name if appropriate:

Our mutual colleague, John Stanovich, felt my skills and abilities would be valuable to your company.

The manager of your San Francisco branch, Pamela Bronson, has suggested I contact you regarding the opening for a _____.

I received your name from Henry Charles last week. I spoke to Mr. Charles regarding career opportunities with _____ and he suggested I contact you. In case the resume he forwarded is caught up in the mails, I enclose another.

Arthur Gold, your office manager and my neighbor, thought I should contact you about the upcoming opening in your accounting department.

If you are writing as the result of a newspaper advertisement, you should mention both the publication and the date—and remember not to abbreviate advertisement to "ad."

I read your advertisement in the Daily Gotham on October 6th and after researching your company, felt I had to write.

I am responding to your recent advertisement offering the opportunity to get involved with automated accounting practices.

In re: Your advertisement in the Columbus Dispatch on Sunday the eighth of November. As you will notice, my entire background matches your requirements.

Your notice regarding a _____ in The Detroit News caught my eye, and your company name caught my attention.

This letter and attached resume is in response to your advertisement in The Boston Globe.

If you are writing to an executive search firm:

(NOTE: In a cover letter to executive search firms, unlike any other circumstance, you *must* mention your salary and, if appropriate, your willingness to relocate.)

I am forwarding my resume to you because I understand you specialize in representing clients in the _____ field.

Please find the enclosed resume. As a specialist in the _____ field I felt you might be interested in the skills of a _____."

Among your many clients may be one or two who are seeking a candidate for a position as a _____.

My salary is in the mid $20's, with appropriate benefits. I would be willing to relocate for the right opportunity.

Step Three

Now turn that interest into desire. First, make a bridge that ties you to a general job category or work area. It starts with phrases like:

I am writing because..

My reason for contacting you is...

This letter is to introduce me and to explore any need you might have
in the _____ area.

...should this be the case, you may be interested to know...

If you are seeking a _____, you will be interested to know...

I would like to talk to you about your personnel needs and my ability
to contribute to your department's goals.

If you have an opening for someone in this area, you will see that my
resume demonstrates a person of unusual dedication, efficiency and
drive.

Then call attention to your merits with a short paragraph that draws attention to one
or two of your special contributions or achievements:

I have an economics background (Columbia) and a strong analytical
approach to market fluctuations. This combination has enabled me
consistently to pick the new technology floatations that are the backbone of the growth-oriented mutual fund.

Similar statements applicable to your area of expertise will give your letter more personal punch. Include any qualifications, contributions, and attributes that qualify you
as someone with talent to offer. If an advertisement (or a conversation with a potential employer) revealed an aspect of a particular job opening that is not addressed in
your resume, it can easily be covered in the cover letter.

I notice from your advertisement that audio and video training experience would be a plus. In addition to the qualifications stated in
my enclosed resume, I have over five years' experience writing and
producing sales and management training materials in both these
media.

Whether you bullet or list your achievements in short, staccato sentences will be
determined in part by the amount of space available to you on the page.

Step Four

Here's where your letter turns that desire into action. You want to make the reader
dash straight to your resume, then call you in for an interview. You achieve this with
brevity.

Your one-page letter shouldn't be longer than four or five paragraphs, or two
hundred words. Leave the reader wanting more. This final step tells the reader that you
want to talk. It explains when, where, and how you can be contacted. Then tell the
reader that you intend to follow up at a certain point in time if contact has not been
established by then. This can encourage a decision on the reader's part to initiate action, which is what you want.

Useful phrases include:

I look forward to discussing our mutual interests further.

It would be a pleasure to give you more data about my qualifications and experience.

I will be in your area around the 20th, and will call you prior to that date to arrange a meeting.

I hope to speak with you further and will call the week of the 20th to follow up.

The chance to meet with you would be a privilege and a pleasure. To this end I will call you on the 20th.

I look forward to speaking with you further and will call in the next few days to see when our schedules will permit a face-to-face meeting.

May I suggest a personal meeting where you can have the opportunity to examine the person behind the resume?

My credentials and achievements are a matter of record that I hope you will examine in depth when we meet.

I look forward to examining any of the ways you feel my background and skills would benefit your organization. I look forward to hearing from you.

Resumes help you sort out the probables from the possibles, but they are no way to judge the true calibre of an individual. I should like to meet you and demonstrate that I have the personality that makes for a successful _____.

My resume can highlight my background and accomplishments. My drive, willingness and manageability, however, can come out only during a face-to-face meeting. With this in mind, I shall call you on the 20th, if I don't hear from you before.

After reading my resume, you will know something about my background. Yet you will still need to determine whether I am the one to help with the current problems and challenges. I would like an interview to discuss my ability to contribute.

I am anxious to meet and discuss any potential opportunities further. I will make myself available for an interview at a time convenient to you.

I expect to be in your area on Tuesday and Wednesday of next week and wonder which day would be best for you. I will call to find out.

With my training and hands-on experience, I know I can contribute to your company, and want to speak with you about it in person. When may we meet?

I feel certain that I can contribute and of my ability to convince you. I look forward to a meeting at your convenience.

You can reach me at 202/555-1212 to arrange an interview. I know that your time investment in meeting with me will be amply repaid.

Thank you for your time and consideration. I hope to hear from you shortly.

May I call you for an interview in the next few days?

I am sure that our mutual interests will be served by speaking further, and am convinced a personal meeting will assure you of my ability, willingness and manageability. I look forward to meeting with you.

A brief phone call will establish whether or not we have mutual interest. Recognizing the demands of your schedule, I will make that call within the week.

As many employed people are concerned about their resumes going astray, you may wish to add:

In the meantime, I would appreciate my application being treated as confidential, as I am currently employed.

Just as you worked to get the opening right, labor over the close. It is the reader's last remembrance of you, so make it strong, make it tight, and make it obvious that you are serious about entering into meaningful conversation.

Writing the Cover Letter

Keep your sentences short—an average of fourteen words per sentence is about right. Likewise, your paragraphs should be concise and to the point. In cover letters, paragraphs can often be a single sentence, and should never be longer than two or three sentences. This makes the page more inviting for the harried reader, by providing adequate white space to ease eye strain.

Short words work best here also. They speak more clearly than those polysyllabic behemoths that say more about your self-image problems than your abilities. A good approach is to think in terms of sending a telegram, where every word must work its hardest.

While abiding by accepted grammatical rules, you should punctuate for readability rather than strictly following E. B. White or the *Chicago Manual of Style*. Get by on commas, dashes—and periods. And inbetween the punctuation marks use the action verbs and phrases that breathe life into your work.

Cover Letter Examples

Notice that the underlined areas come directly from the previous examples. You too can write a dynamite cover letter with the old "cut and paste" technique. Then all you have to do is make the minor adjustments necessary to personalize your letter:

Wilfred Corrigan   November 16, 1988
1234 La Cienega Blvd
Los Angeles, CA 93876

Dear Mr. Bell,

Recently I have been researching the leading local companies in data communications. My search has been for companies that are respected in the field, and who provide on-going training programs. DataLink Products keeps coming up as a top company.

I am an experienced voice and data communications specialist with a substantial background in IBM environments. If you have an opening for someone in this area you will see that my resume demonstrates a person of unusual dedication, efficiency, and drive.

My experience and achievements include:

* The complete redesign of a data communications network, projected to increase efficiency company wide some 12%;

* The installation and troubleshooting of a Defender II call-back security system for a dial-up network.

I enclose a copy of my resume, and look forward to examining any of the ways you feel my background and skills would benefit DataLink Products. While I prefer not to use my employer's time taking personal calls at work, with discretion I can be reached at 213/555-5555 to initiate contact. Let's talk!

Yours truly,

Wilfred Corrigan

Wilfred Corrigan

In response to an advertisement, here is an example using a different selection of phrases.

Joyce Carlton   November 16, 1988
376 Jaguar Lane
Sunnyside, NY 11104

Dear Ms. Pena,

I have always followed the performance of your fund in Mutual Funds Newsletter.

Recently, your notice regarding a Market Analyst in Investors Daily caught my eye— and your company name caught my attention, because your record over the last three years shows exceptional portfolio management. With my experience with one of your competitors, I know I could make significant contributions.

I would like to talk to you about your personnel needs and how I would be able to contribute to your department's goals.

As an experienced market analyst I have an economics background and a strong analytical approach to market fluctuations. This combination has enabled me to consistently pick the new technology flotations that are the backbone of the growth-oriented mutual fund.

For example, I first recommended Fidelity Magellan six years ago. More recently, my clients have been strongly invested in Pacific Horizon Growth (in the high-risk category), and Fidelity Growth and Income (for the cautious investor).

Those following my advice over the last six years have consistently outperformed the market.

I know that resumes help you sort out the probables from the possibles, but they are no way to judge the personal calibre of an individual. I would like to meet with you and demonstrate that, along with the credentials, I have the personality that makes for a successful team player.

Yours faithfully,

J. Carlton

Joyce Carlton

The Executive Briefing

Here is a variation on the traditional cover letter. It has been developed most effectively by the recruiting fraternity for use in relation to a specific opening.

Behind the executive briefing is the belief that the initial resume screener might have little understanding of the job in question. So a format was developed that dramatically increased the odds of your resume getting through to the right people. In addition, it customizes your general purpose resume to each specific opening you discovered.

It looks like this:

EXECUTIVE BRIEFING

for a

CREDIT/LOAN SUPERVISOR

as advertised in the Gotham Daily News

Jane Swift
9 Central Avenue
Mesa, AZ 85201
602/964-5652

To help you evaluate the attached resume and manage your time effectively today, I have prepared this executive briefing. It itemizes your needs on the left and my skills on the right. The attached resume will give you additional details.

Job Title:	My Current Title
CREDIT AND LOAN SUPERVISOR	CREDIT AND LOAN SUPERVISOR
Required Experience:	Relevant Experience
* 5 years in consumer banking	5 years with a major Arizona consumer bank
* Knowledge of Teller Operations	4 years in Teller Operations, as teller and supervisor
* 3 years Consumer Loans and Mortgage Loans	5 years Consumer & Commercial and Mortgages
* Extensive Customer Service Experience	4 years in customer service. Reviewed as "having superior communication skills."

An executive briefing sent with a resume provides a comprehensive picture of a thorough professional, plus a personalized, fast, and easy-to-read synopsis that details exactly how you can help with an employer's current batch of problems.

The Broadcast Letter

The broadcast letter is nothing but a simple variation on the cover letter. All the information you would need is available to you from the achievements section of your questionnaire. The intent is to get around sending a resume. Practically speaking, it can often get you into a telephone conversation with a potential employer, but that employer is usually likely to request a proper resume before seeing you anyway. While a broadcast letter might have a place in your campaign, do not use it as a resume substitute. Here is an example of a broadcast letter, in this instance sent in response to a blind newspaper advertisement:

Dear Employer,

For the past seven years I have pursued an increasingly succesful career in the sales profession. Among my accomplishments I include:

SALES

As a regional representative, I contributed $1,500,000, or 16% of my company's annual sales.

MARKETING

My marketing skills (based on a B.S. in Marketing) enabled me to increase sales 25% in my economically stressed territory, at a time when colleagues here were striving to maintain flat sales. Repeat business reached an all-time high.

PROJECT MANAGEMENT

Following the above successes, my regional model was adopted by the company. I trained and provided project supervision to the entire sales force. The following year, company sales showed a sales increase 12% above projections.

The above was based and achieved on my firmly held zero price discounting philosophy. It is difficult to summarize my work in a letter. The only way I can think of providing you the opportunity to examine my credentials is to talk with each other. I look forward to hearing from you.

Yours sincerely,

Chester Philbin

As you can see, the letter is a variation on a theme, and as such might have a place in your marketing campaign.

Here is an example of a cover letter sent as a result of a conversation.

Dear Ms. Alden,

I am writing in response to our telephone conversation on Friday the 10th, regarding a new- and used-car sales management position.

With a successful track record in both new- and used-car sales, and as a sales manager, I believe I am ideally suited for the position we discussed. My exposure to the different levels of the sales process (I started at the bottom and worked my way up), has enabled me to effectively meet the challenges and display the leadership you require.

I am a competitive person professionally. Having exercised the talents and skills required to exceed goals and set records as a Sales Manager, I believe in measuring performance by results.

I would appreciate your consideration for a meeting where I could discuss in more detail my sales and management philosophy, and capabilities. Please call me at your earliest convenience to arrange a personal meeting.

Sincerely yours,

George Ruffino

Finally, here is an example of the somewhat different cover letter you would send to a corporate headhunter:

Dear Mr O'Flynn,

As you may be aware, the management structure at XYZ Inc. will be reorganized in the near future. While I am enthusiastic about the future of the company under its new leadership, I have elected to make this an opportunity for change and professional growth.

My many years of experience lends itself to a management position in any medium-sized service firm, but I am open to other opportunities. Although I would prefer to remain in Detroit, I would be amenable to relocation if the opportunity warrants it. I am currently earning $65,000 a year.

I have taken the liberty of enclosing my resume for your review. Should you be conducting a search for someone with my background—at the present time or in the near future—I would greatly appreciate your consideration. I would be happy to discuss my background more fully with you on the phone or in a personal interview.

Very truly yours,

James Wolenik

Chapter Eight: What Do You Do With It?

Creating one of the best resumes in America is a major part of your job hunt, but, nevertheless, only a part. It won't get you a job by sitting on your desk like a rare manuscript. You have to *do* something with it.

Companies are always looking for employees. Even a company with no growth rate can still be expected (based on national averages) to experience a 14% turnover in staff over the course of a year. In other words, every company has openings, and any one of those openings could have your name on it.

The problem is, you won't have the chance to pick the very best opportunity unless you check them all out. There is a six-pronged approach that every intelligent job hunter will use to cover all the bases. This process will incorporate different ways to use

- Newspapers

- Employment Agencies

- Executive Recruiters

- Vocational and College Placement Offices

- Business and Trade Publications

- Personal and Professional Networking

Newspapers

A first step for many is to go to the want ads and do a mass mailing. But beware. If this is the first idea that comes to *your* mind, hitting the want ads will probably be at the front of everyone else's mind, too.

A single help-wanted advertisement can draw hundreds of responses. And that's not counting all the other unsolicited resumes that come in every day. So your approach must be more comprehensive than that of the average applicant. The following tips might be helpful:

- Newspapers tend to have an employment edition every week (usually Sunday, but sometimes mid-week), when in addition to their regular advertising they have a major drive for help-wanted ads. Make sure you always get this edition of the paper.

- Look for back-issues. Just because a company is no longer advertising does not necessarily mean that the slot has been filled. The employer may well have become disillusioned and gone on to hire a professional recruiter to work on the position.

- Cross-check the categories. Don't rely solely on those ads seeking your specific job title. For example, let's say you are a graphic artist looking for a job in advertising. Any advertising or public relations agency with any kind of need should be flagged by you. On the basis that they are actively hiring at the moment, simple logic leads you to the conclusion that their employment needs are not restricted to that particular title.

Newspapers represent an important part of your marketing campaign; you should follow up all your resumes with a phone call about a week after they have been sent.

Employment Agencies

There are essentially three categories: State employment agencies, private employment agencies, and executive recruiters.

State Employment Agencies

These are funded by the state's labor department and typically carry names like State Employment Security, State Job Service, or Manpower Services. The names vary, but the services remain the same. They will make efforts to line you up with appropriate jobs and will mail resumes out on your behalf to interested employers who have jobs listed with them. It is not mandatory for employers to list jobs with state agencies, but more and more are taking advantage of these free services. Once the bastion of minimum-wage jobs, positions listed with these public agencies can reach $50-60 thousand a year for some technical positions.

If you are moving across the state or across the country, your local employment office can plug you into a computer bank accessing major employers on a national basis (often referred to as a national "job bank"). Insiders agree, however, that it can take up to a month for a particular job from a local office to hit the national system. The most effective way to use the service is to visit your local office and ask for an introduction to the office in your destination area.

Private Employment Agencies

Here we have a definitely for-profit sector of the employment marketplace. There are some major questions that you should get answered before signing up with any particular agency. Chief among them: Are the fees to be paid by the client or by you as the job candidate? The answer distinguishes employer paid fee (or EPF) agencies from applicant paid fee (or APF) agencies. In all but the most dire emergencies you are strongly recommended to work only with EPF companies. Apart from the expense, you simply don't want to be known as someone who has to pay to get a job.

You are best advised to call first, verify the fee status, and then visit. Be prepared to leave a copy of your resume for their files and for possible review by interested clients.

Here are some practical ways for you to check on the professional standing of your agent. Be sure to ask:

- When was the firm established? If the company has been in town ever since you were in diapers, the chances are good that it is reputable.

- Is the agency a member of the state employment association? State associations have strict codes of behavior and ethics, and provide ongoing training for their members. And as in all industries, people and companies who are actively involved in enhancing their profession invariably have an edge on the competition.

- Does your particular agent have a CPC designation? That stands for Certified Personnel Consultant, a title achieved only after considerable time and effort. Employment consultants with this designation come straight from the top drawer, so you can trust them and should listen attentively to their advice.

- Is the agency part of a franchise chain or independent network? Knowing this can be valuable to you, because both types of organization provide considerable training for their associates, a feature that can enhance the level of service you receive. In addition, other members of the network may have a job suitable for you if the one you've located doesn't.

Finally—don't get intimidated. Remember you are not obliged to sign anything. Neither are you obliged to guarantee an agency that you will remain in any employment for any specified length of time. Don't get taken advantage of by the occasional rogue in an otherwise exemplary and honored profession.

Executive Recruiters

These people rarely deal at salary levels under $70 thousand a year. All the above advice regarding employment agencies applies here, although you can take it for granted that the headhunter will not charge you a fee. He or she will be more interested in your resume than in seeing you right then and there, unless you match a specific job the recruiter is trying to fill for a client. Executive recruiters are far more interested in the employed than in the unemployed. An employed person is less of a risk (headhunters often guarantee their finds to the employer for up to a year) and constitutes a more desirable commodity. Remember, these people are there to serve the client, not to find you a job. They neither want nor expect you to rely on them for employment counseling, unless they specifically request that you do—in which case you should listen to them closely.

Vocational and College Placement Offices

If you're leaving school, you should take advantage of this resource. (If you don't, you're crazy.) Many of the larger schools have alumni placement networks, so even if you graduated some time ago, you may want to check with the alma mater and tap into the old-boy and old-girl network.

Business and Trade Publications

Two uses here. The articles about interesting companies can alert you to growth opportunities, and the article itself can provide a neat little entre' in your cover letter. Of course, there's also the welcome fact that most of these magazines carry a help-wanted section.

Networking

A fancy word from the Seventies that means talking to everyone you can get hold of in your field, whether you know them or not.

The Encyclopaedia of Associations (published by R.R. Bowker) tells you about associations for your profession. Networking at the meetings and using an association's directory for contacts are wise and accepted uses of membership.

At the Library

The business reference section can give you access to numerous research books that can help, including:

- Standard and Poor's
- The Thomas Register
- The National Job Bank
- The Directory of Directories

Follow-Up

It is no use mailing off tens or even hundreds of resumes without following up on your efforts. If you are not getting a response with one resume format, you might want to consider redoing it another way, as discussed in Chapter Five. Of course, in doing so, you should never mention your previous submission. Be satisfied with one of your baits catching a fish.

Always take five or six copies of your resume with you to interviews. Often you can attach it to those annoying application forms and then just write on the form "See attached resume." You can have one on your lap during the interview to refer to, as the interviewer does.

It is always wise to offer copies to subsequent interviewers. This is because they have very often been inadequately briefed and may have no idea about your background and skills. It's also a good idea to leave extra copies of your resume behind with managers for their personal files (which travel with them through their careers from company to company). That person may not need you today, but could come up with a dream job for you sometime in the future. I know of people who have landed jobs years later as a result of a resume left judiciously with the right person. Who is the right person? Potentially, anyone who holds on to your resume.

The job you ultimately accept may not be your picture of perfection. Nevertheless, any job can lead to great things. You can make the opportunities for yourself in any job if you make the effort. A job becomes what you choose to make it.

In the job hunt there are only two kinds of "yes" answers: Their "yes-we-want-you-to-work-for-us", and your "yes-I-can-start-on-Monday". The joy is in the hunt, with every "no" bringing you closer to the big "yes". Never take rejections of your resume as rejections of yourself; just as every job is not for you, you aren't right for every job. Keep things in perspective.

Good luck!

Chapter Nine:
The Resumes

And now, without further ado...the stars of our show. The resumes on the following pages are based on the genuine articles, the ones that really did the trick for someone who had to translate their fantastic skills and background into a single, compelling document. Whether or not your background is represented in the following sample, use the resumes reproduced here as a starting point for composing your own.

Which Style Is Best For You?

The first three resumes in this section are based on the completed questionnaire you'll find on page 211. Each has been written in a different format—chronological, functional, and combination—to show the dramatic changes you can achieve by using each of the recommended resume styles.

Jane Swift, 9 Central Avenue, Quincy, MA 02269. (617) 555-1212

SUMMARY: Ten years of increasing responsibilities in the employment services industry. Concentration in the high technology markets.

EXPERIENCE: Howard Systems International, Inc. 1985-Present
Management Consulting Firm
Personnel Manager

Responsible for recruiting and managing consulting staff of five. Set up office and organized the recruitment, selection and hiring of consultants. Recruited all levels of MIS staff from financial to manufacturing markets.

Additional responsibilities:
* coordinated with outside advertising agencies
* developed P.R with industry periodicals -- placement with over 20 magazines and newsletters
* developed effective referral programs -- referrals increased 32%

EXPERIENCE: Technical Aid Corporation 1977-1985
National Consulting Firm. MICRO/TEMPS Division

Division Manager 1983 - 1985
Area Manager 1980 - 1983
Branch Manager 1978 - 1980

As Division Manager, opened additional West Coast offices Staffed and trained all offices with appropriate personnel. Created and implemented all divisional operational policies responsible for P & L. Sales increased to $20 million dollars, from $0 in 1978.

* Achieved and maintained 30% annual growth over 7 year period.
* Maintained sales staff turnover at 14%.

As Area Manager opened additional offices, hiring staff, setting up office policies and training sales and recruiting personnel.

Additional responsibilities:
* supervised offices in two states
* developed business relationships with accounts -- 75% of clients were regular customers.
* client base increased 28% per year.
* generated over $200,000 worth of free trade journal publicity.

As Branch Manager, hired to establish the new MICRO/TEMPS operation. Recruited and managed consultants. Hired internal staff. Sold service to clients.

EDUCATION: Boston University
B.S. Public Relations, 1977

Jane Swift
9 Central Avenue
Quincy, MA 02269
(617) 555-1212

OBJECTIVE: A position in Employment Services where my management, sales and recruiting talents can be effectively utilized to improve operations and contribute to company profits.

SUMMARY: Over ten years of Human Resources experience. Extensive responsibility for multiple branch offices and an internal staff of 40+ employees and 250 consultants.

SALES: Sold high technology consulting services with consistently profitable margins throughout the United States. Grew sales from $0 to over $20 million a year.

Created training programs and trained salespeople in six metropolitan markets.

RECRUITING: Developed recruiting sourcing methods for multiple branch offices.

Recruited over 25,000 internal and external consultants in the high technology professions.

MANAGEMENT: Managed up to 40 people in sales, customer service, recruiting, and administration. Turnover maintained below 14% a "turnover business"

FINANCIAL: Prepared quarterly and yearly forecasts. Presented, reviewed and defended these forecasts to the Board of Directors. Responsible for P & L of $20 million sales operation.

PRODUCTION: Responsible for opening multiple offices and accountable for growth and profitability. 100% success and maintained 30% growth over 7 year period in 10 offices.

**WORK
EXPERIENCE:**

1985 to Present HOWARD SYSTEMS INTERNATIONAL, Boston, MA
National Consulting Firm
Personnel Manager

1978-1985 TECHNICAL AID CORPORATION, Needham, MA
National Consulting & Search Firm
Division Manager

EDUCATION: B.S., 1977, Boston University

REFERENCES: Available upon request.

EMPLOYMENT SERVICES MANAGEMENT

Jane Swift
9 Central Avenue
Quincy, MA 02269
(617) 555-1212

OBJECTIVE:

Employment Services Management

SUMMARY: Ten years of increasing responsibilities in the employment services marketplace. Concentration in the high technology markets.

SALES: Sold high technology consulting services with consistently profitable margins throughout the United States. Grew sales from $0 to over $20 million a year.

PRODUCTION: Responsible for opening multiple offices and accountable for growth and profitability. 100% success and maintained 30% growth over 7 year period in 10 offices.

MANAGEMENT: Managed up to 40 people in sales, customer service, recruiting, and administration. Turnover maintained below 14% a "turnover business". Hired Branch Managers, Sales and recruiting Staff throughout United States.

FINANCIAL: Prepared quarterly and yearly forecasts. Presented, reviewed and defended these forecasts to the Board of Directors. Responsible for P & L of $20 million sales operation.

MARKETING: Performed numerous market studies for multiple branch openings. Resolved feasibility of combining two different sales offices. Study resulted in savings of over $5,000 per month in operating expenses.

EXPERIENCE: Howard Systems International, Inc.   1985-Present
                 Management Consulting Firm
                 Personnel Manager

                 Responsible for recruiting and managing consulting staff of five. Set up office and organizied the recruitment, selection and hiring of consultants. Recruited all levels of MIS staff from financial to manufacturing markets.

                 Additional responsibilities:

                 * developed P.R with industry periodicals -- placement with over 20 maganizes and newsletters
                 * developed effective referral programs -- referrals increased 320%

                 Technical Aid Corporation   1977-1985
                 National Consulting Firm.   MICRO/TEMPS Division

                 Division Manager   1983 - 1985
                 Area Manager   1980 - 1983
                 Branch Manager   1978 - 1980

                 As Division Manager, opened additional West Coast offices Staffed and trained all offices with appropriate personnel. Created and implemented all divisional operational policies. Responsible for P & L. Sales increased to $20 million dollars, from $0 in 1978.

                 * Achieved and maintained 30% annual growth over 7-year period.
                 * Maintained sales staff turnover at 14%.

                 As Area Manager opened additional offices, hiring staff, setting up office policies, training sales and recruiting personnel.

                 Additional responsibilities:
                 * supervised offices in two states
                 * developed business relationships with accounts -- 75% of clients were regular customers.
                 * client base increased 28% per year.
                 * generated over $200,000 worth of free trade journal publicity.

                 As Branch Manager, hired to establish the new MICRO/TEMPS operation. Recruited and managed consultants. Hired internal staff. Sold service to clients.

EDUCATION: B.S., 1977, Boston University

Jane Swift
9 Central Avenue
Baltimore, MD 21207
(301) 555-1212

CAREER OBJECTIVE To work in an Accounting/Business position that offers advancement opportunities.

EMPLOYMENT
1986-Present   An established health care Co.
                            ACCOUNTANT

- Responsible for Accounts Payable for 5 companies
- Responsible for Payroll of all companies. Time saving of 11% across the board
- Maintain personnel records
- Administrator of Employee Benefits
- Prepare Cost Analysis for development projects of Real Estate Division
- Assisted in implementation of computerized accounting system

1983-1986   National Service Corporation, Baltimore
                            JUNIOR ACCOUNTANT

- Preparation of month-end reports
- Processing of all expense reports, educational assistant applications, and accounts payable
- Processing of Region Payroll

1980-1983   CASSON INC., Baltimore
                            ADMINISTRATIVE SECRETARY

- Data collection and analysis for market research projects
- Project budgeting and cost containment
- Processed departmental accounts payable and expense reports
- Maintained market research library
- Assisted with implementation of and transition to computerized system

EDUCATION   University of Baltimore, (Baltimore, MD)
                            Associate in Science Degree
                            Major: Accounting

Accounting Customer Service Specialist

Jane Swift
9 Central Avenue
MERRICK, NY 11516
(516) 555-1212

OBJECTIVE

A challenging position, utilizing abilities developed through my experience and education, with the opportunity for professional growth based on performance.

EXPERIENCE

1986-Present   CHUBB INSURANCE COMPANY, CARLE PLACE, NY
Accounting Customer Service Specialist
-Prepared daily correction for suspense reports
-Balanced billing statements
-Handler customer inquiries concerning coverage changes, rebills, renewal rates and reinstatement procedures
-Prepared requisitions for overpayment refund checks
-Investigated premium posting errors

1982-1986   NATIONAL CREDIT UNION, BROOKLYN, NY
Accounting Service Coordinator
-Consolidated daily transactions of all Automatic Teller machines in the state (50)
-Processed applications for the ATM
-Transferred funds through First Carolina Corporation for external users

Member Service Representative/Teller
-Opened new accounts for members; handled inquiries
-Participated in cross-selling the services of the Credit Union
-Performed data entry of daily loan transactions
-Provided paying/receiving functions
-CRT and 10 key calculator skills

1979-1982   IBM CORPORATION, PORT WASHINGTON, NY
Wordprocessor
-Performed word processing, typing, filing, and other general office duties; set appointments

EDUCATION

Bachelor of Business Administration
North Carolina Central University, Durham, NC.

Accounting Clerk

Jane Swift
9 Central Avenue
Huntington Valley, PA 19006
(215) 555-1212

JOB OBJECTIVE   To pursue an accounting career

EXPERIENCE   ACCOUNTS PAYABLE CLERK. Fast Markets, Huntington Valley, PA.

6/85 to Present
* Recorded daily accounts receivable checks. Normal day: 50 checks with total value of $70,000
* Computerized complete accounts payable system, for a saving of 80 man hours a week
* Computed daily bank deposits
* Reconciled monthly bank statements
* Recorded general ledger entries
* Maintained automated billback accounts receivable system including daily data entry into IBM Systems 38 computer
* Coordinated regular meetings with wholesaler and merchandise representatives to reconcile their accounts receivable

1/79 to 6/85   ACCOUNT SERVICE REPRESENTATIVE. Sales Department

* Performed general clerical duties
* Catalogued product orders for military accounts
* Responsible for customer order status information

04/74 to 01/79   ACCOUNTING OFFICE CLERK. Jack Rabbit Foods, Huntington Valley, PA.

* Responsible for all basic accounting functions: Coding and distribution of invoices, classified transactions and processed distribution center invoices

EDUCATION   HOLYOKE COMMUNITY COLLEGE, Holyoke, MA. Degree in Accounting. Graduated 9-73.

REFERENCES   Available upon request

Accounts Payable Supervisor

Jane Swift
9 Central Avenue
Detroit, MI 48204
(313) 555-1212

OBJECTIVE

To obtain a supervisory position in an Accounts Payable department that will utilize accounting skills and provide the opportunity for professional development

EXPERIENCE
Feb. 1985 to
Present

Sweetrest Beds   Detroit, MI
Accounts Payable Supervisor

* Supervised accounts payable personnel and reviewed their daily work.
* Utilized IBM System 11 computer system for various accounting functions.
* Managed, calculated, and maintained weekly payroll records for 300 employees
* Prepared weekly Federal, FICA, and State withholding deposits.
* Delegated monthly bank reconciliations and reviewed work.
* Prepared monthly account analysis (detailing and verifying the general ledger balance sheet accounts).

Aug. 1976 to
Feb. 1985

Wagstaff Kitchens   Detroit, MI
Accounts Payable Clerk

* Prepared and entered vendor invoices into IBM and Wang computers
* Responsible for writing checks for vendors and operating expenses
* Handled all vendor inquiries and reconciled vendor statements
* Designed a more efficient vendor information apron, which was approved by management
* Analyzing weekly vendor aging reports
* Prepared monthly insurance expenses for payroll
* Trained new personnel
* Assisted in the supervision of departmental staff

EDUCATION

City University Detroit, MI. Bachelor of Science in Business Administration, May 1985. Major: Accounting

Expenses financed through part-time employment, financial aid, and parental contributions

INTERESTS

Personal Computing. Chess

REFERENCES

Available upon request

Administrative Assistant

Jane Swift
9 Central Avenue
GLENDALE, CA 91209
(818) 555-1212

SUMMARY OF EXPERIENCE

Degenhart Aluminum Recycling Co., Glendale CA. Personnel Assistant (7/83 - present)

Administrative Assistant to the Personnel Manager. Served as liaison between company and employees. Duties included:

Taking shorthand and the use of the IBM Displaywriter Word Processor.

Dictaphone transcription, preparation of correspondence.

Assisting employees in field locations in complying with administrative procedures.

Maintaining up-to-date employee records and compiling reports, working directly with employees and answering questions regarding benefits, medical claims and assisting them with necessary paper work.

Employer comments: "Extremely organized ... exceedingly proficient"

Degenhart Aluminum Recycling Company. Benefits Coordinator (1978-1983)

Processed medical claims for employees. Began employment as a statistical typist and was promoted to the Claims Department.

Employer comments: "Willingness to work till the job is done . . . Easy to work with"

Bank of Glendale, Mastercard Division, Glendale, CA. Typist (1977-1978)

Dictaphone transcription for the Collection Department.

Employer comments: "Tactful and considerate . . . takes initiative."

EDUCATION

Priory High School, Philadelphia, PA: June 1969

Admissions Representative

James Sharpe
9 Central Avenue
Philadelphia, PA 19046
(215) 555-1212

CAREER OBJECTIVE

A position in education, recruitment, or personnel development.

CENTRAL PHILADELPHIA COLLEGE, PA. ADMISSIONS REPRESENTATIVE. 1980 - Present

*Performed telemarketing procedures to set private interviews, schedule career workshops in 100 area high schools.

*Conducted personal interviews with prospective students.

*Designed and implemented career education and motivation workshops for high school students. Lead to 8% application increase.

*Designed brochures and handouts to accompany workshop presentations.

*Exceeded lead generation quota by 16%

*Successfully addressed parent and student groups on Financial Aid.

*Coordinated student-faculty participation in recruitment activities.

CHARLES HAID, M.D., PHILADELPHIA. SECRETARY. 1978-1979

*Coordinated a number of administrative activities in this busy practice; implemented office automation system ahead of schedule, increasing personal and office productivity.

TEACHER OF ART AND MUSIC, MADISON, WI. 1976-1977
*Successfully taught in elementary and secondary schools in the midwest for ten years, specializing in art and music.

EDUCATION:
B.A. Notre Dame in Liberal Arts cum laude.
Computer Science Studies. Philadelphia College

EXTRACURRICULAR
Speakers Bureau, 82-88, Philadelphia College

Applications Management Specialist

James Sharpe
9 Central Avenue
Cleveland, OH 44116
(216) 555-1212

HARDWARE/
SOFTWARE: IBM 3083, 4341, 370/158, OS/MVS, VM/CMS, COBOL, EASYTRIEVE, CULPRIT, EDIT, XEDIT, VSAM, ISA's OSCARS, GENESYS PAYROLL/PERSONNEL

EXPERIENCE:

Cleveland Savings. Team Leader. 8/83 to Present

Responsible for the management and direction of 10 Programmers and Programmer/Analysts, and for the maintenance and implementation of all Financial systems. Duties include work prioritization, project assignment, and coordination. Supervisory responsibilities include hiring/termination, performance appraisal, budget administration and annual staffing projections. Heavy user interface with all levels of management. Promoted to Team Leader in 1987.

> *Accomplishments:*

- Reduced initial workload from 62 outstanding projects to 12, by completing 106 projects in 24 months.

- Direct a 25-member Project Team for the installation of On-Line Securities Control and Reporting System (OSCARS).

- Directed a 10 member Project Team in the successful regeneration of the Genesys Software System Payroll/Personnel System.

Ohio Federal Savings. Programmer. 4/81 to 8/83

Participated in the ongoing maintenance of the FSS Demand Deposit Account and Certificate of Deposit systems. Methods and Procedures Analyst. As support for data processing, researched and wrote extensive analytical reports, provided cost/benefit analysis and hardware performance reports to upper management.

EDUCATION:

John Carroll University: B.A. - Business Administration, 1981

Applications Programmer/Analyst

James Swift
9 Central Avenue
Wilmington, MA 01887
(617) 555-1212

SUMMARY: A seasoned P/A with experience comprising all facets of the applications development cycle, working in on-line, database, and batch processing environments.

HARDWARE/
SOFTWARE: 43XX, OS/MVS/XA, DOS/VSE, COBOL, PASCAL, BASIC, CICS, DL/1, VSAM, ICCF, ROSCOE, EASYTRIEVE, SORT/MERGE, MSA A/P, TSO/SPF, EDGAR, VOLLIE

EXPERIENCE: *1st Bank of Boston. Programmer/Analyst. 1/88 to Present*

Responsible for installation and maintenance of MSA Accounts Payable System. Member of a team that designed and coded a front-end system to MSA Payroll that allowed online daily input, employee inquiry and accompanying batch reports including labor distribution. Analyzed, coded and maintained COBOL and CICS Command Level programs, applications included: Profit Sharing, General Ledger, Gross Profit Forecasting, Billing and Sales Reporting.

Shearson. Programmer/Analyst. 10/83 to 1/88

Promoted to Programmer/Analyst after eight months as a Documentation Analyst. As a Programmer, was a member of the Customer Support Group for the Integrated Financial Information System. Resolved client software problems, coded and installed software modifications at client sites. Analyzed and coded program modifications as required. Responsibilities included: Reconciliation, Accounts Payable and General Ledger.

EDUCATION: *Drexel University*
B.S. - Accounting/Computer Systems Management (May, 1982)

Assistant Manager Trainee

James Sharpe
9 Central Avenue
Overland Park, MA 66212
(913) 555-1212

PROFESIONAL OBJECTIVE

An administrative/managerial position in which I can utilize my skills and abilities.

EXPERIENCE
1986 - Present

UNION SAVINGS BANK   Overland Park, MA

Administrative Assistant/Assistant Manager Trainee
Monitored cash flow and alarm systems, supervised Customer Service Department, Payroll Department and tellers. Regularly reported to the Assistant Vice President. Fifteen people reported to me on a daily basis. Assumed responsibilities of Branch Manager in the absence of the Assistant Vice President.

Supervisor to Customer Service Department
Drafter weekly and monthly financial reports, monitored safe deposit boxes, handled new accounts for branch, updated department personnel on bank policies and products. Five people reported to me.

Customer Service Representative
Provided customers with information, bank products and services such as brokerage accounts, certificates and savings and checking Accounts.

1980 - 1986

TELECOMMUNICATIONS, INC.   Overland Park, MA
Administrative Assistant
Worked closely with the editor and staff of Computer Magazine, a monthly computer magazine. Responsibilities included interacting with readers and vendors, handling correspondence, making travel arrangements, assisting editors and reporters in story research as well as other projects.

EDUCATION
9/85 - 12/85

WORD PROCESSING
Overland Adult Education Program
Comprehensive word processing course. Hands-on-experience with Digital Rainbow and Apple IIE (Bank Writer and PFS:WRITE).

PERSONAL

Member of Massachusetts coalition for literacy. Enjoy reading, scuba diving, camping. Well-developed ability to delegate assignments and convey job goals. Work well with people.

REFERENCES

Available upon request.

Associate (Legal)

Jane Swift
9 Central Avenue
New York, NY 10017
(212) 555-1212

EDUCATION

Legal: Columbia Law School, J.D., 1984: Grade Average: B+

Bar Admission: New York, 1984; United States Federal District Court (Manhattan), 1985.

College: Yale University, B.A. with Honors, 1981. GPA: 3.5

Secondary: Waldorf School, 1974-1977

EMPLOYMENT

1986-Present

Associate with Skasky Bryant of New York. General corporate representation of early-stage, growth-oriented hi-tech companies, usually in computer industry. Concentration on negotiation and drafting of technology-related contracts, distributorship, proprietary rights and employee agreements. Regular involvement in private financings of high-technology companies.

September, 1984-March, 1986:

Associate with Kliernan, Peabody & Schraft of New York. General corporate work, acquisitions, private financings, negotiation and drafting of computer and other contracts. Experience in real estate and litigation.

Summer, 1983:

Summer associate with deJong & Kelsey of San Jose, CA. Hi-tech corporate representation.

Summer, 1982:

Intern with Environmental Protection Bureau of New York State Attorney General's Office.

PERSONAL DATA

Skills: Scientific background; familiar with Spanish and Chinese.

Automobile Salesperson

JAMES SHARPE
9 Central Avenue
Melrose, MA 02176
(617) 555-1212

OBJECTIVE: New Car Sales Manager

PRINCIPAL SKILLS:

New Car Sales Manager; Automobile/Professional Sales and Finance

EXPERIENCE: TOYOTA OF MELROSE. 1985 - Present. **Sales Manager**

Initially hired as **Salesman.** Proved professional skills and talents for working and dealing effectively with the public and desire and ability in training and influencing others. Promoted (after one year) to **Sales Manager.** Responsible for 24 new and used-car sales.
Achievements include:

◇ New Car sales increase 12% in 1986, 27% in 1987.
◇ Staff turnover reduced 14%.
◇ Cost of sales remained constant.

MELROSE AUTO SALES. 1979 - 1985. **Salesman**

Responsible for new and used-car sales. Earned "Salesman of the Year" awards, 1985 and 1986. Record-holder for:
Most Cars Sold in One Month
Most Cars Sold in One Year
Most Board Gross in One Month
Most Board Gross in One Year

CAREFREE ADVERTISING AGENCY. 1975 - 1979
Direct Commercial Advertising Sales

U.S. ARMY. 1971 - 1975
Helicopter Flight Engineer
Served in Vietnam, April 1972 to November 1973. Awarded the Bronze Star Medal, the Air Medal and the Army Commendation Medal. Honorable Discharge.

EDUCATION: University of Massachusetts
Completed 30 credit hours: College Accounting I and II, Personnel Management and related courses.

Professional Courses and Seminars:
Dr. Norman Vincent Peal—Self-Starter Sales
Zig Zigler—Motivation and Sales
Jackie Cooper—Making the Sale/Closing the Sale
Toyota Sales Society

REFERENCES: Furnished upon request.

Automotive Management Specialist

James Sharpe
9 Central Avenue
Raleigh, NC 27612
(919) 555-1212

Employment Experience

Service Manager. Capucci Chevrolet. Raleigh, NC. 1984-present.

Supervised 22 mechanics, customer service relations, processing of warranty claims. I/M program coordinator, trained mono-lingual mechanics, safety coordinator, pay sublet repair shops, authorized check requests, analyzed employee production, produced reports for entire car dealer department operations.

Adjunct Professor. Raleigh Community College. 1977-1985

Teacher of Automotive Technology for A.A.S. (34 credits). Prepare lessons and evaluate class performance. Spanish and English courses.

Licenses

North Carolina State Inspectors License, Type F & E
New York City Board of Education Auto Mechanic

Certificates

Certificate of Competence: Sponsored by the National Institute for Automotive Service Excellence of Washington, D.C. (Certification)

Front End	Engine Performance
Brake Systems	Heating & Air Conditioning
Electrical Systems	Engine Tune-Up

Certificate of Training: Given by the Consumer Relations and Service Staff of General Motors Corporation
Driveability diagnosis Computer Command Control
Electronic Fuel Injection
Computer Command Control Engine Performance

Certificate of Training: Given by the Monroe Auto Equipment Company
Principles of Shock Absorbers
Theory of Automotive Suspension

Certificate of Training: Given by the United Delco Training Program
Hydraulic System and Disk Brakes
Power Service Emissions Control
Power Service Fuel Systems

Education
Raleigh Community College
A.A.S. Electrical Technology

References furnished upon request.

Bank Teller

James Sharpe
9 Central Avenue
Kansas City, MO 64108
(816) 555-1212

OBJECTIVE: Seek a responsible position with growth opportunities in the field of Financial Management.

PROFESSIONAL EXPERIENCE:

May 1985 to Present

FIRST SAVINGS BANK   Kansas City, MO
Bank Teller
Duties include computing figures with speed and accuracy, maintaining proper activity in customer accounts, operating computer to retrieve processed data, controling and supervising large amounts of cash flow, and obtaining accountability of transactions.

January 1984 to May 1985

NATIONAL WESTMINSTER BANK (internship)   Kansas City, MO
Assistant to Retirement Accounts Manager
Duties include recording of contributions to new and existing accounts, assisting customers with information regarding benefits of IRA's and KEOGH's calculating specific year-to-date interest and tax deduction advantages, assisting manager with form procedures to complete transactions.

Special research project as to the feasibility of funding retirement accounts with Zero Coupon Bonds obtained currently by brokers and anticipating the participation of Finalcial Institutions, specifically banks.

EDUCATION: B.B.A., City University College, May 1985. Concentration in Management Techniques, interest in Finance.

SPECIAL ACTIVITIES: Student Academic Affairs Committee, attention to improving balance within the academic environment at the college.

REFERENCES: Furnished upon request.

Bank Wire Transfer Clerk

Jane Swift
9 Central Avenue
Memphis, TN 38119
(901) 555-1212

EXPERIENCE:

NATIONAL BANK OF MEMPHIS   October 1984 - present

Wire Transfer Clerk
* Settled money position with the Federal Reserve Bank
* Recorded information from customers (telephone) for outgoing wires
* Prepared proof entries for Federal account
* Sent out wires on wire machine
* Documented all incoming and outgoing wires

File Maintenance (Data Entry)
* Input all new accounts, CD's, address changes
* Set up new ports for new accounts, TransFund card, safety deposit accounts

Safe Deposit Box
* Controlled customer access to boxes
* Prepared and sent billings and accepted payments

1st TENNESSEE BANK   June 1980 - October 1984

Wire Transfer Clerk
* (Same duties as listed above)

Customer Service/Bookkeeping
* Responded to telephone inquires
* Filing checks, preparing statements, return items

Proof Department
* Operated proof machine
* Sent out clearing house and balanced cash letters

BOWDLER CLOTHING STORES   January 1978 - June 1980

Cash Office Clerk
* Balanced cash from registers and safe
* Balanced Visa and MasterCard
* Rolled coins and ordered money for safe

EDUCATION:

MEMPHIS JUNIOR COLLEGE

* Completed coures in Principles of Banking, and data processing.

References Available Upon Request

Banking Portfolio Manager

SUMMARY

A track record of outstanding performance in the sophisticated environments of Trust and Investment banking. Management of both personal and institutional portfolios with total values exceeding $700 million. An adept analyst of such diverse industries as energy, metals, automobile, insurance, banking, electrical and consumer goods.

OBJECTIVE

An opportunity where a professional whose successful loss control/profit preservation approach to portfolio management can make a meaningful contribution.

CAREER HIGHLIGHTS

An Investment Banking Company: Vice President, Institutional Portfolio Management. 1984-Present.

Heads investment management activities of the firm's 170-account Kansas office. Reporting to Chairman. Created more effective marketing and management of large accounts, by initiating a program which resulted in:

* Upgrading and expansion of professional staff
* Personal management of firm's 17 largest accounts.
* Effective supervision of all staff activities and performance.
* Elevation to position as member of Corporate Board of Directors and Chair of Investment Strategy and Policy Group.

Kansas Trust Company: Vice President & Senior Portfolio Manager. 1980-1984.

Managed a broadly diversified account base of over 395 personal and institutional accounts with total value in excess of $950 million. Improved performance of accounts supervised, shortened turn-around time of customer requests for investment reviews, cementing relations with clients. Developed effective computerized methods for rapid analysis of investment diversification.

* Program consistently outperformed the S&P index, distilled stock guidance list of 500 firms to a value-oriented 20-35 companies.
* Reduced turn-around time on investment reviews by 30%.
* Reduced time spent in review analysis by 25% while improving review quality.

Morgan Guaranty (New York): Portfolio Manager. 1977-1980.

Initially recruited as a Senior Investment Analyst in the energy stock area, was promoted to Portfolio Manager within 10 months.

* Hired, trained, supervised and directed activities of additional analysts in related research coverage.
* Dramatically reduced energy stock holdings in November 1980, a move which produced sizable realized capital gains while avoiding the sell-off which followed.
* Instituted automation and software for analytical staff. Increased the number of potential investment opportunities by 21% without additional cost.

EDUCATION AND PERSONAL

MBA, Columbia Business School   Finance and Marketing
MA, John Carrol University   Economics
BA, John Carrol University   Economics

Willing to relocate. References are available upon request

Bookkeeper

James Sharpe
9 Central Ave
Wilmington, DE 19850
(302) 555-1212

OBJECTIVE

To pursue a career in the accounting field, utilizing my proven capabilities in payroll, general bookkeeping, cost and accounting.

EXPERIENCE

Leader Instrument Corporation, Wilmington, DE
Bookkeeper, 1/84 - Present

Responsibilities include accounts receivable, accounts payable and payroll. Reconcile bank statements and accounts. Maintain depreciation schedules and monthly analysis. Prepare payroll for 100 employees, W-2 forms, quarterly returns and other related payroll functions. Calculate employee sales commissions and employee production bonuses. Involved in major W.P. conversion and upgrade

John Dalig, Wilmington, DE
Payroll Clerk, 9/81 - 1/84

Responsibilities included payroll returns, writeups, reconcilations, analysis work and depreciation schedules. Figured timecards (overtime and shift); checked suspect entries with applicable supervisor. Performed other payroll related activities. Assisted in the supervision and training of all new department members

The Chubb Life Insurance Company, Wilmington, DE
Cost Accounting Systems Coordinator, 9/79 - 6/81

Controlled all input and analyzed all output to the functional Cost System and EDP Cost Allocation System. Prepared analytical information based on functional costs; calculated and distributed expense accounts departmentally. Reconciled the system to all company ledgers to assure the system was in complete balance

EDUCATION

Wilmington Junior College, Wilmington, DE. Business Administration, 1970

REFERENCES

Furnished upon request

Broadcast Management Professional

Jane Swift
9 Central Avenue
Clifton, NJ 07013
(201) 555-1212

**PROFESSIONAL
INTEREST**   Marketing Management, Broadcast Management

**WORK
EXPERIENCE**

MARKETING DIRECTOR - A major provider of satellite communications services for broadcasting and private business networks. 1986-present.
* Member of policy making corporate management team.
* Manage company's strategic position to effectively penetrate the multimillion-dollar corporate/organizational private satellite network market.
* Increased corporate visibility in the satellite industry through developing corporate image, producing new and comprehensive sales materials, and strengthening public relations and advertising efforts in trade magazines.
* Identified new market segments and reached these segments with successful direct-mail campaigns.

PRODUCT DEVELOPMENT MANAGER - Viacom International, Los Angeles, CA. 1985-86.
* Supervised market research, market segmentation analysis, and product management.
* Designed and assisted in the composition of a Prospectus for use in attracting potential investors in the Company.

MARKETING VICE PRESIDENT'S ASSISTANT - KNEW TV & AM, Los Angeles, CA. 1980-1985
* Supervised all activities, (i.e., tours, printed and electronic advertising, hiring, catering, etc.) for successful two-week Grand Opening of multimillion-dollar Headquarters.
* Planned and supervised all marketing and promotional activities at KNEW.

PUBLIC RELATIONS DIRECTOR - KPIX, Los Angeles, CA. 1977-80.
* Supervised and designed corporation's first external newsletter for use in market development.
* Designed photo layout for use in advertising and press releases.

**ADDITIONAL
INFORMATION**

* Speak, read and write Spanish fluently.
* Vice-President, American Marketing Association, NY Chapter, 1984-85
* Publications Vice-President, MBA Student Association.

EDUCATION   **M.B.A,** Marketing Emphasis, Northwestern University. 1977.

B.A., Public Relations, John Carrol University. 1975.

REFERENCES   Available upon request.

Buyer

James Sharpe
9 Central Ave
Manhattan, NY 10012

EXPERIENCE

3/86 - Present   Ohrbach's, (New York, NY) **Buyer,** *Boyswear*

Responsible for purchasing boyswear sold in boys departments at 45 stores chainwide, with yearly sales exceeding $5.5 million. Branch managers report to this position.

* Visit wholesale showrooms on a weekly basis.

* Analyze daily sales data and inventories to plan promotions and make adjustments.

* Prepare and maintain budgets. Redistribute merchandise between stores.

* Travel to branch stores to direct departmental start-ups and solve problems.

* Train and evaluate assistant buyers.

2/85 - 3/86 **Assistant Buyer,** *Silverware/Cookware/Junior Knits*

Promoted through three different lines. Consistently exceeded quota.

* Assisted buyers in selection of merchandise.

* Prepared orders, budgets, and inventories.

* Planned and created newspaper advertisements.

* Organized and promoted annual Housewares Exposition.

8/83 - 2/85 **Sales Manager**

* Managed four separate departments in two stores, exceeded projections 14%.

* Trained, scheduled, and supervised salespeople, turnover dropped 20%.

* Met daily sales quotas, handled all merchandising.

EDUCATION

B.A. Merchandising: New York Fashion Institute of Technology (1982)

All education self-financed through working in Manhattan retail outlets throughout college years.

Capital Equipment Salesperson

6 Central Avenue
Beaverton, OR 97005
(503) 555-1212

JAMES SHARPE

OBJECTIVE   Challenging position in MARKETING/SALES offering an opportunity for growth.

SUMMARY   B.S. Degree in Business Administration plus six years' experience marketing capital equipment to the health care market.

EMPLOYMENT EXPERIENCE

A Major U.S. multinational corporation in the life sciences industry. 1986-Present
Northwest Territory Area Sales Representative.
Responsibilities include marketing X-ray equipment and ancillary products through X-ray dealers and OEM's to the Health Facilities market in western states. Routine interface between end-users, planning consultants, architects, and dealer salespeople on systems sale.

Beale Company, Sacramento CA. 2/80-3/86
Western Sales Representative.
Responsible for marketing sterilizers and surgical lighting fixtures directly to Health Facilities market and through dealer network to the laboratory market. Achievements include:
* Rookie of the Year Award, 1982
* Million Dollar Club (annual sales exceed 1 million) '82, '83 & '85
* Summit Club '82, '83, '84 & '85
* Hawaii Sales Contest Winner, 1983; Gold Ounce Sales Winner, 1984

10/1977-2/1980   Mead Paper, Dayton, OH
Major U.S. multinational corporation in the forest products industry.
Corporate Trainee.
Started as Assistant to the Division Manager in Dayton working primarily on an inventory control system prior to computer start-up. Accepted transfer to strengthen sales force with responsibilities for 42 retail accounts and business development within a specific territory.
* Doubled sales volume within six months.

EDUCATION
1973-1977   Bachelor of Science, School of Business Administration
Major concentration in Marketing with emphasis on Promotional Strategies and Consumer Behavior.
University of Connecticut, Storrs, CT

PERSONAL AND PROFESSIONAL REFERENCES AVAILABLE UPON REQUEST

Chemical Salesperson

James Sharp
9 Central Avenue
DALLAS, TX 75379-1906
(214) 555-1212

OBJECTIVE:

To work for a growing company where my background in sales can be used to good advantage.

SUMMARY OF
EXPERIENCE:

Wide-ranging background in agricultural chemicals and fertilizer sales. Experience gained through employment with large chemical companies. I feel that being a strong self-starter has helped me obtain many of my goals.

EMPLOYMENT HISTORY:

A Major Chemical Company, Dallas, TX 1982-Present:
A sales representative for an agricultural chemical company. Sales territory has achieved 18%-23% sales increases over past four years. Responsibilities include: Sales forecasting, sales planning and inventory control.

Promote impregnation of agricultural chemicals on dry fertilizer. In 1987 I increased sales with those 22 dealers that impregnated by 28%.

Conduct 30 to 40 grower, dealer and distributor meetings a year.

Work one-on-one with 20% of the dealers that do 80% of the business, presenting marketing and incentive programs. Sales increase of 2.4 million dollars over last three years.

I designed a marketing program offering free insecticide banders for those customers using our product. This idea is now a national program.

Made presentations to sales force on impregnation, complaint handling, and setting up dealer calls.

Chevron, Tulsa, OK. 1975-1982
Sales representative calling directly on large plantations and dealers. Increased sales 25% in 1979, 24% in 1980, 33% in 1981, and 20% in 1982.

EDUCATION:

North Carolina State University, B.S Agriculture

SPECIAL TRAINING:

Training offered by major agricultural chemical companies.

Agsell
Professional Selling Skills
Action Management
Customer Complaints as Sales Opportunities

Claims Representative

Jane Swift
9 Central Ave.
Sacramento, CA 95691
(916) 555-1212

Objective:	Seeking a position utilizing my extensive knowledge and successful experience in planning, organizing and following-up multi-faceted, complex activities; and a position offering opportunities for personal contribution and professional growth.

SUMMARY OF QUALIFICATIONS

Experience: Offering comprehensive experience and expertise in the following areas of responsibility:

* Extensive experience planning, organizing, evaluating and following-up varied responsibilities in a timely and complete manner.

* Proficient in developing excellent relationships with clients and consultants.

* Experienced in knowledge of and in analyzing provisions and exclusions of policies in order to decide eligible benefits.

* Skilled at organizing work and resolving problems which arise in day-to-day activities.

* Record of conscientious application, reliability and loyalty in past positions.

EXPERIENCE HIGHLIGHTS

1985 to Present **Claims Representative**
Farmers Fund Insurance Company, Sacramento, CA

Responsible for meeting with policyholders, claimants, and attorneys to examine, evaluate and decide upon claims for property damage and personal injury.

* Planning, organizing, evaluating and approving up to 100 active claims in process. Evaluating claims in relation to all provisions and exclusions of the policy.

* Taking statements of witnesses and performing on-site inspections. Analyzing reports and statements of policy-holders, witnesses and claimants.

* Receiving and evaluating medical reports. Performing analytical reports of bodily injury claims.

* Negotiating claims settlements with individuals and attorneys.

1983 to 1984 **Management Trainee**
PizzaTime Theaters, Sacramento, CA

Participated in Management Training Program and assisted in interviewing, hiring, training and supervising personnel. Managed operations in absence of Manager.

1982 to 1983 **Administrative Assistant**
Eastern Illinois University, Charlestown, IL.

Responsible for assisting Alumini Fund Director in fund-raising projects. Maintained daily and monthly reports of fund-raising activities. Organized and coordinated meetings and luncheons.

Education:	BACHELOR OF ARTS DEGREE, Eastern Illinois University, Charleston, IL. 1983. Majored in Speech Communication/Business Management.
Licenses:	Casualty License including Auto Physical Damage and Liability and General Liability issued by Texas Board of Insurance.
Strengths:	Highly motivated and goal-oriented, accurate, thorough and precise in attention to details. Excellent analytical and organizational skills. Major strength is completing multi-faceted tasks within time constraints allotted. Skilled in public relations, loyal, dependable and willing to do whatever is needed to meet established goals.

REFERENCES AND FURTHER INFORMATION FURNISHED UPON REQUEST

Compensation/EEO Specialist

OBJECTIVE

A career opportunity in Personnel Management that will implement skills gained through successful, broad-based experience, and utilize expertise in organization and management, ability to structure a responsive, well-accepted personnel function.

SKILL SUMMARY

Compensation

Responsible for all phases of salary administration. Developed, implemented complete compensation programs including international, sales and executive compensation. Formulated basic concepts, prepared proposal for corporate approval, formalized policies and procedures.

Designed and participated in wage and salary surveys, evaluated the comparative level of overall compensation.

Modified and/or developed salary ranges. Established and administered salary increase forecasts, merit and promotional budgets. Initiated programs and criteria for employee performance evaluation.

Administered salaries correlating potential percent of increase with quality of performance. Developed bonus and incentive plans as appropriate. Hands-on knowledge of the Hay system, factor-comparison and point-factor systems, etc. Designed, developed, implemented a Personal Data system and a Skills Inventory system.

Equal Employment Opportunity

Developed, revised, updated, and implemented Affirmative Action Plans according to company requirements.

Conducted compliance reviews, worked with inspection teams or individuals; negotiated where necessary.

Maintained appropriate files on protected classes in company; reviewed new job requisitions to insure equal considerations and promotion commensurate with performance. Organized and ran training sessions for supervisors and managers on training and upgrading of minorities.

Employment

Directed all aspects of professional, technical and administrative recruiting. Administered employee relations programs; counseled employees concerning personal or job-related problems, established effective relocation procedures.

Training, Development/Manpower Planning

Introduced management-by-objective concepts, developed programs and processes, implemented system on national basis.

Identified manpower planning needs, designed and implemented staffing and forecasting plans, using top-to-bottom participative process integrated with sound business strategy. Designed and taught a variety of programs for all levels of management, exempt and non-exempt personnel.

Benefits

Developed requirements, selected and administered group life health insurance plans, long-term disability, travel and accident programs. Negotiated with insurance carriers to secure competitive benefit levels at lowest possible cost.

COMPANY AFFILIATIONS

1982-present	Coca-Cola, Atlanta, GA
	Director of Personnel
1977-1982	CITIBANK, New York, NY
	Manager, Salary Administration
1974-1977	LAURA ASHLEY, Trenton, NJ
	Manager, Salary Administration
1966-1974	PALL CORPORATION, Long Island, NY
	Personnel Manager

PROFESSIONAL ASSOCIATIONS

American Society for Personnel Administration
American Compensation Association
New York Personnel Management Association
New York Compensation Association

EDUCATION

New York University, 1962-1966

Commercial Lender

James Sharpe
9 Central Avenue
Chapel Hill, NC 27514
(919)555-1212

EXPERIENCE:

November 1983
to Present: Current employer is a top financial institution

March 1985
to Present: <u>Assistant Vice President - Commercial Lending</u>

                     Handling a $15-million portfolio consisting of
                     approximately 210 accounts. Portfolio consists of: Accounts
                     Receivable, Real Estate, Airplane, Inventory, and Equipment
                     Lending. Dealing with credit of $10,000 to $1 million.

1983 to 1985   <u>Credit Analyst - Loan Review</u>

                     Credit Analysis, Documentation Review, Loan Department
                     Reports, Review of Documentation in Credit Files, Credit
                     Quality.

1978 to 1983   <u>Assistant Bank Examiner   N.C. Bank Regulatory
                     Commission</u>

                     Examination of banks, conducted appraisal and review of
                     loans. Audited internal controls and records. Review for
                     compliance and consumer regulations.

EDUCATION:

                     Masters Degree in Business Administration - Finance
                     N.C. State University

                     Bachelor of Science Degree - Psychology
                     N.C. State University

**CONTINUING
EDUCATION:**   Bank Auditing & Accounting School
                     Trust Examination School
                     Compliance School (Consumer Regulations)
                     Loan Review & Analysis School

REFERENCES: ·Available Upon Request.

Computer Operator

Jane Swift
9 Central Avenue
Costa Mesa, CA 92626
(714) 555-1212

CAREER OBJECTIVE: A challenging position with the opportunity for advancement in the field of data processing.

WORK EXPERIENCE:

3/87 - present

Wells Fargo. Costa Mesa, CA
COMPUTER OPERATOR

Duties include running daily routines, maintaining data files, generating and distributing computer reports and performing backups on an IBM System 36. Additional duties include file and system documentation on an IBM Personal Computer.

2/83 - 3/87

San Bruno Savings & Loan. San Bruno, CA
DATA ENTRY OPERATOR

Duties include inputting data for accounts payable, accounts receivable, general ledger journal entries, financial statements, and budgets. Additional responsibilities include word processing using an IBM Personal Computer.

7/79 - 2/83

San Bruno Savings & Loan
SECRETARY

Duties included typing case reports, answering the telephone, and filing. Backup duties as computer operator for the IBM System 34, IBM System 36, and IBM Series One. Also fill in as receptionist and switchboard operator when needed.

EDUCATION:

9/86 - present

UCLA
Currently attending classes at night in pursuit of a Computer Science Degree.

References available on request.

Credit/Collections Clerk

JANE SWIFT
9 CENTRAL AVENUE
ANDOVER, MA 01810
(617) 555-1212

OBJECTIVES

A challenging position in office administration with a growing company, where my dedication and attention to detail will create opportunities for growth.

EXPERIENCE

DAN RIVER, September 1983 to present
CREDIT/COLLECTIONS ADMINISTRATOR

Collect monthly percentage of receivables established by corporate headquarters, research billing errors and adjust customer accounts. Personnally reviewed all major accounts and adjusted ratings. Customer review. May 1985 to present

BILLING/DATA ENTRY

Updating customer master file, maintaining individual customer account records, review work orders to generate invoices and statements. Coordinate and order materials and supplies. September 1983 to May 1985

THE CREDIT BUREAU. FT WAYNE. IN 1981 - 1983
CREDIT CLERK

Responsible in area of collection for physicians, attorney status, typing statements and cases dealing with insurance, social security and medicare

SHERATON HOTEL, ANDOVER JULY 1980 TO AUGUST 1983
CLERK/AUDITOR

Nightly audit and deposits. Take and confirm reservations, organize group tours, greet and register guests, handle complaints, show and rent apartment, take inventory, order supplies

EDUCATION

ANDOVER COMMUNITY COLLEGE 1978. Accounting

REFERENCES available upon request

Credit/Loan Supervisor

Jane Swift
9 Central Avenue
Mesa, AZ 85201
(602) 555-1212

OBJECTIVE
A supervisory position providing the opportunities to further develop and apply skills and experience in bank operations.

SUMMARY OF EXPERIENCE
Nearly three years, progressively responsible experience in banking; familiarity in teller operations with the subsequent transfer to loan operations, including consumer loans, mortgages, and commercial loans. Extensive customer service experience.

EXPERIENCE
April 1986 - Present
Mesa Savings, Mesa, AZ. Assistant Credit Supervisor, Commercial Loan Department
* Responsible for the smooth day-to-day running of department of 5
* Review new loans for application to computer system and subsequent balancing
* Handle customer inquiries and solve billing problems
* Assist in billing, receipt, application to computer of payments
* Prepare various reports and information for loan officers
* Participate in the training and development of staff
* Assist supervisor with all other pertinent duties
* Participated in a recent computer conversion

April 1984 - April 1986
Bank of Arizona, Flagstaff, AZ. Assistant Commercial Loan Operations Manager. April 1986

* Manager a staff of 3; assisted in their training and development
* Oversaw daily functions, including customer servicing, billing, and computer input and its subsequent balancing
* Controlled collateral areas; reviewed loan documentation
* Prepared various reports and information for loan officers
* Organized a tickler and filing system

Loan Operations Clerk (March 1984 - April 1985)
* Performed various duties assigned by the Loan Manager, including credit investigations and inquiries, computer input and settlement, maintenance of files, and typing of reports and letters

EDUCATION
American Institute of Banking, Worcester, MA.
Athol - Warren Koch High School, Flagstaff, AZ. Graduated 1983

Credit Manager

James Sharpe, 9 Central Avenue, Novi, MI 49050. (313) 555-1212

OBJECTIVE

A key management position offering decision-making responsibilities where I can implement skills gained through successful experience in Credit/Sales Management

SUMMARY OF QUALIFICATIONS

Operate successfully with firm conviction that all cash due is collectable. Research, using all available information; quickly, accurately appraise a situation; exercising sound judgment, implement an effective course of action.

Develop excellent rapport with customers while significantly shortening pay-out terms, through application of problem-solving techniques. Evaluate their sales performance in terms of potential; offer suggestions, alternatives regarding financing/merchandising; perform on-the-spot negotiations; turn impending loss into profit.

- Personally salvaged and increased sales with two multi-million dollar accounts by providing remedial action for their sales/financial problems.

- Brought previous collection turns from 85 days to present average of 39 days, thereby turning sales into cash in less than 40 days. Reduced interest expense by more than half a million dollars.

- Operated with 1/10th of 1% bad debt loss while maintaining,increasing sales activities with marginal accounts, some rated as low as EE-3.

- Maintained close working relationship with National Sales Manager and field. Initiated direct communication line between credit and sales via collections route, using the collections procedure as a means to generate sales.

EXPERIENCE

HAGERTY CORPORATION, Novi, MI
Consumer Electronics
National Credit Manager. Have developed close working relationships with national chains: K-Mart, Woolco, Zayres, G.C. Murphy, Macy. Travel extensively to customers, strengthening sales. 1986-present

VICTORIA'S SECRET, San Francisco, CA
Lingerie
Controller. Restructured operations, reorganized record-keeping, reduced staff by 11. Initiated and installed internal audit system tying together billing, shipping purchasing and receiving. Involved in heavy usage of EDP systems. 1981-1986

BURLINGTON INDUSTRIES, Elizabeth, NJ
Home Furnishings
Credit Manager. Responsible for all accounting services for 2200 active accounts. Clerical staff of 10. 1979-1981

RESORT WEAR, New York, NY
Fashion
Accountant. Initiated and installed cost controls from piece to finished goods. 1971-1981

EDUCATION

Georgia Institute of Technology (New York, NY)
B.A. Degree, Accounting (1970)

New York Institute of Finance (New York, NY)
Special courses in Financial Statement Analysis and Auditing.

Customer Service Manager

JAMES SHARPE, 9 CENTRAL AVENUE, MIAMI,, FL 33152. (305) 555-1212

EXPERIENCE

CUSTOMER SERVICE MANAGER. A TELECOMMUNICATIONS
SATELLITE COMPANY   5-86 to Present

Hired and developed a staff of forty people to service the customer service needs of our highest revenue commercial accounts. Maintained an account retention percentage of 99%, while keeping revenue loss through credits to less than 2%.

CUSTOMER SERVICE - TELEMARKETING MANAGER
MCI – S.E Region Customer Service Center, Miami, FL.

3-84 to 5-86

Hired and developed a staff of sixty customer service - telemarketing representatives and supervisors.

Managed a mixture of inbound and outbound call activities with job responsibilities including: sales, customer service, customer correspondence and special projects.

Responsible for a budget of close to one million dollars.

CUSTOMER SERVICE SUPERVISOR
NYNEX, New York, NY   1-83 to 3-84

Supervision of a division customer service staff. Responsibilities include: providing support for our sales force and sales management, implementing new policy and procedures for customer service and monitoring to see that all our sales and service objectives are met.

CUSTOMER SERVICE REPRESENTATIVE
NYNEX   6-78 to 1-83

Involved in all aspects of customer-service including: answering questions, problem solving, interfacing with our sales force and working with new customers to implement SPRINT services.

EDUCATION.

B.A. 1978. Florida State University.

TRAINING.

Leadership and Management of Change. Results Oriented Management. Managing Management Time.

REFERENCES AVAILABLE ON REQUEST

Data Processing Consultant

Jane Swift
9 Central Avenue
King of Prussia, PA
(215) 555-1212

HARDWARE:	IBM 3031, IBM 4341, UNIVAC 1100/60/80, UNIVAC 90/30, Burroughs 3500/4700, NCR Century/Criterion, Honeywell 6000, IBM and IBM Compatible Microcomputers
O/S:	VM/CMS, OS/MVS, TSO, OS/1100, MCP, GCOS, PC-DOS, MS-DOS, NOVELLE, ALLOY ATNX
SOFTWARE:	EDITOR-1100, TIP-1100, DPS-1100, DMS-1100, QLP-1100, CTS, DML, DDL, SDDL, SSG, GSA, IRU, ECL, JCL, JES2
LANGUAGES:	COBOL, BASIC, GW-BASIC, MS-BASIC, R:BASE 5000/SYSTEM V, TAS DBMS, CONDOR II, DBASE III, NEAT/3, ADA
EDUCATION:	M.S Computer Systems, May 1980 San Jose State, CA

Consulting projects include the following:

Analyzed the requirements of a Professional Property Management firm, to determine the lowest cost multi-user configuration, based upon existing and projected requirements. Developed, acquired and installed all hardware, peripheral equipment and software.

Performed a workflow analysis of the procedures for filling customer orders at a Valve Manufacturer's finished goods warehouse. Upon completion, presented to corporate management a formal report of the workflow and current operating procedures.

Developed an interactive multi-user system for a Structural Steel Fabricating Company, to calculate the weight of finished goods based upon dimensions listed on architectural drawing.

Developed the software modules for an interactive database for a Slate Roofing Company, based upon specifications provided by prime contractor.

For a major bank performed trade-off studies to identify capabilities suitable for replacement with commercially available off-the-shelf products vs. being developed internally. Projected lines of code estimates for modules being rewritten in Ada.

For County Government responsible for the conversion of COBOL applications from a Univac 90/30 to a Univac 1100/60. Developed JCL runstreams for all systems converted.

FURTHER INFORMATION AND REFERENCES AVAILABLE UPON REQUEST

Data Processing Supervisor

James Sharpe
9 Central Avenue
Lakewood CO 80228
(303) 555-1212

OBJECTIVE:

To make a contribution using my proven abilities with MAPPER Run Design, Microcomputers and Mainframes.

EXPERIENCE HIGHLIGHTS:

A COMPUTER PERIPHERAL MANUFACTURER, Denver, CO. 1980 - Present

DATA PROCESSING SUPERVISOR: Responsible for overseeing the work of seven (7) full-time and three (3) part-time employees. Coordinated, controlled and directed the ordering, use and maintenance of Unisys Equipment. Ensured accuracy and security wih all Data Entry and Output.
Accountable for the maintenance, operation, and performance of the UNIDATS Data Communications Network for Denver and all outside users. Responsible for the MAPPER site-coordinator and user community.

TECHNICAL PROGRAMMER: Responsible for the operation of DP Center. Extensive system programming in Assembler for the Univac 9300. Position required thorough knowledge of communications equipment.

EDUCATION:

UNIVERSITY OF SOUTH FLORIDA - St. Petersburg, Florida
B.A. Business Administration
Major: Management (with emphasis on programming languages)

AFFILIATIONS:

Member - Data Processing Management Association:
1984-85 Director
1983 Student Chapter Chairperson
1982 Program Chairperson.

PERSONAL ATTRIBUTES:

I am accustomed to accepting responsibility and delegating authority, and am capable of working with and through people at all levels. Am able to plan, organize, develop, implement and supervise complex programs and special projects. Have a good sense of humor and a personal dedication to producing timely, cost-effective results.

Database Administrator

Jane Swift
9 Central Avenue
New York, NY 10021
(212) 555-1212

SUMMARY. Twelve years' data processing experience in a Mainframe/Transaction Database environment that includes 8 years as Corporate Database Administrator.

HARDWARE & SOFTWARE. Univac 1108, 1100/40, 60, 62, 80; IBM 33X, 43X ANSI COBOL, Univac ECL, Symbolic Stream Generation, Assembler, COBOL Database Manipulation Language, Text Editor, CTS, Query Language, DDL, SDDL, Transaction Programming Language, SCIP/SCOP, BASIC, ASSEMBLER, MS-DOS.

COURSES. UNIVAC -DDL, SDDL, QLP, SSG, COBOL Database Manipulation Language, Database Design Assembly Language Programming, CTS Users Workshop, Systems Support Programming, Transaction Processing Programming

1982 to present   *SULIKAN COPPER. Database Administrator*

* Database usage monitoring, database maintenance and sizing, database reorganizations. Also schema/subschema enhancements

* Designed and successfully implemented schema and subsystem flow for the Order Entry Subsystem

* Designed and successfully implemented Corporate Micro Computer Hardware and Software Standards, saving the company over $40,000 in 1986

* Maintained communications network for over 150 terminals

* Corporate Micro Computer Hardware/Software Support Manager for an installed base of 400 personal computers

* Developed and maintained Cobol/Transaction/Database applications programs

1980-1982   *INCO INC. Database Administrator*

* Translated logical design through physical design into IMS control blocks.

* Monitored and tuned IMS and CICS/IMS applications.

* Forecasted capacity requirements for new IMS or CICS releases.

* Assisted Applications by converting existing files to IMS Fastpath.

* Designed and implemented numerous utilities which automated many DBA tasks.

1976 to 1980   *REDMARK RETAILERS. Programmer/Analyst*
Support of large online/batch purchasing system

References available on request.

Dietitian

Jane Swift
9 Central Avenue
Middleburg Heights, OH 44130
(216) 555-1212

JOB OBJECTIVE: To provide quality nutritional care to individuals through clinical or community responsibilities.

EXPERIENCE:
August 1984-
Present   *Dietary Director*, Middleburg Community Hospital (Middleburg, OH)
Supervise in-depth nutritional assessment of patients on hyperalimentation, formulation of classes on weight reduction, diabetes, and geriatric nutrition. Chief of Staff describes the improvement in the quality of patient care and food served in the hospital as "nothing short of spectacular."

October 1985-
Present   *Consultant Dietitian* (part-time), Veterans Hospital. (Cleveland, OH)
Developed standards for nutritional care, assisted the dietary director in preparation of the policy and procedure manual, conducted routine clinical duties.

April 1981-
August 1984   *Clinical Dietitian/Assistant Director of Dietary*, St John's Hospital, (Cleveland, OH.)
Developed cost-effective nourishment center, produced videotaped modules on weight reduction, diabetic, and low-sodium diets. Established nutritional care standards for hepatic disease for use by local dietitians.

EDUCATION:

M.S. in Nutrition, Michigan State University
B. S. in Dietetics, Michigan State University
Dietetic Internship, Veterans Administration Hospital, Detroit, MI

REFERENCES: Available upon request

Director of Development

Jane Swift
9 Central Avenue
Houston, TX 77031
(713) 555-1212

EXPERIENCE

Director of Development: Performing Arts School of Houston. 1986 - Present
*Created an annual giving program to raise operating funds. Raised $2,000,000.
*Target, cultivate and solicit sources including individuals, corporations, foundations, state and federal agencies. Raised $1,650,000.
*Raised funds for development of the Performing Arts School facility, capital expense, and music and dance programs. Raised $6,356,000.
*Cultivated long term public relations through effective advertising and public awareness campaigns.

Assistant Development Director: Performing Arts School of Houston. 1979-1986
*Involved with all phases of fund-raising and public relations.

*Researched and targeted potential donors, wrote proposals, contributed fundraising campaign ideas. Initiated the corporate sponsor program. Program continues to generate over $1,000,000 a year.

*Assisted in the cultivation of effective media coverage through writing and distributing press releases and public service announcements. Print and electronic media coverage increased 136%.

Medical Administrative Assistant: University of Texas Medical Center (Houston), 1976 - 1979

Managed three physicians' offices by coordinating schedules, handling patient billing, transcribing dictation, typing. Performed library research. Edited book chapters, manuscripts, and grants. Created and prepared slides for seminars. Composed administrative correspondence. Organized meetings.

ADDITIONAL AFFILIATIONS

* Consultant, Media Relations, Lone Star Singers
* Member, Houston Area Women in Development
* Chairperson, Public Relations Committee, Center for the Performing Arts Campaign
* Advanced Word Processing Certificate, 1986

EDUCATION:
University of Texas at San Antonio. B.A. Music (1976).

Director of Medical Records

JANE SWIFT
9 CENTRAL AVENUE
WATERBURY, VT 05676
(802) 555-1212

EMPLOYMENT HISTORY:

SISTERS OF MERCY HOSPITAL. Waterbury, VT. Director, Medical Records   *1983-present*
Plan, organize, direct, and control the activities of two supervisors and fifteen employees in a medical record department servicing a 320 bed non-profit teaching hospital with an annual rate of 12,000 patient discharges, 17,388 emergency service visits, and 29,723 out-patient and clinic visits.
Accomplishments:

◇ Reduced backlog of $1.2 million in suspended billing and a three month backlog in coding within first three months of assumption of department in 1983.

◇ Eliminated a backlogged in-house transcription service with a direct-dial contract transcription service resulting in improved turnaround time, better quality transcription. Reduced loss of transcription from 20% to negligible rate.

WATERBURY GENERAL HOSPITAL. Waterbury, VT. Assistant Director Medical Records 1976-1983
assisted in planning, organizing, directing, and controlling the activities of five employees in a medical record department servicing a 267 bed proprietary hospital with an annual rate of 8,000+ patient discharges.
Accomplishments:

◇ Opened the Medical Record Department in this new hospital, 1976.

◇ Planned departmental layout, staffing, policies and procedures for new department.

◇ Prepared department for initial Medicare, state licensure, and JCAH surveys for Medical Record Services, Medical Audit Program, Utilization Review and Library Services.

PROFESSIONAL ORGANIZATIONS

American Medical Record Association
Risk Management Association
DRG Management Association

EDUCATION

Vermont State University. Certification: Medical Record Administration
Connecticut State University: B.A. 1976

Electrical Design Engineer

Jane Swift
9 Central Avenue
Wilton, CT 21234
(203) 555-1212

CAREER
OBJECTIVE: Development and Design of Digital and Analog equipment.

SUMMARY: Experienced with TTL, ECL, GaAs, programmable arrays, and microprocessors. Familiar with RS-232, IEEE-488, and manchester code interfaces. Analog design included Op-Amps, D/A'S, A/D'S, multiplexers, and sample/holds. Secret clearance.

EXPERIENCE:
1986- Present   *ELECTRICAL ENGINEER (SIKORSKY, CT)*

Designed digital and analog equipment for Avionic Fuel Measurement and Management Systems. Prime flight hardware and support test equipment designs include:

Analog Signal Conditioner - Unit to condition analog and digital signals provided to flight system computers. Design employed D/A converters, active filters and digital logic.

Digital Display Indicator - Indicator displayed fuel quantity information to ground crew. Design consisted of LCD displays, digital logic and self-contained power supply. Dealt with small packaging requirements.

Analog Tester - Designed support test equipment to perform Acceptance Tests on Analog Signal Conditioner.

Digital Tester - Designed support test equipment to perform Acceptancy Test on Digital Display Indicator

1979 - 1986   *DESIGN ENGINEER (SIMMONDS PRECISION, VT)*

Member of circuit design group. Responsible for the design and debug of various analog and digital circuits/systems. Responsibilities included:

Video processing portion of a radar pulse processing system. Included work with video amplifiers, track/hold amplifiers,and the high-speed A/D convertors, as well as TTL (ALS, FAST, LS), and other high-speed logic.

A servo-controller that used programmable array logic, TTL, Op-AMps, and D/A convertors.

A spread spectrum radio that used high-speed TTL (FAST), programmable array logic, and a 16-bit microprocessor, with a custom interface and a RS-232 interfact.

EDUCATION: Old Dominion University, Norfolk, VA.
B.S.E.E., cum laude.

Electrician

James Sharpe
9 Central Avenue
Metairie, LA 70002
(504) 555-1212

SUMMARY
Master Electrician (licensed in Louisiana A-15346). Experienced in all types of electrical work - residential, commercial, industrial, electrical construction, and estimating. Six years management experience as a Foreman.

EXPERIENCE
1985 to present
Cajun Electric—Metairie. Master Electrician
Responsible for all sales, estimating, work scheduling, billing, ordering of parts and equipment, maintenance of inventories, and customer service. Projects have included complete wiring of a manufacturing business after relocation, new home construction, repair of equipment, building additions. Have worked as a contractor and subcontractor.

1985
Industrial Light—New Orleans. Journeyman Electrician
Foreman on medium-sized projects, with crews of 2 to 10. Scheduled the work, checked quality and productivity, provided layouts and supervision.

1982
Prudhomme & Sons—New Orleans. Journeyman Electrician
Crew member on construction of the New Orleans Sheraton.

1980
Bechtel—Saudi Arabia. Journeyman Electrician
Worked on a nuclear power plan (heavy industrial project), where safety and reliability were extremely important.

1981 to 1982
Tujaques—New Orleans. Journeyman Electrician
A variety of commercial and industrial projects (hospital, high rise condominiums, office-hotel complex).

TRAINING
Louisiana Technical College, New Orleans
Certificate in Completion of Apprenticeship program

PERSONAL
Willing to travel, relocate

References Available

Engineering Secretary

Jane Swift
9 Central Avenue
Denver, CO 80223

EXPERIENCE: <u>1983 - Present, MOUNTAIN BELL, DENVER, ENGINEERING SECRETARY</u>

Engineering Department Secretary, responsible to 11 managers: Typing, vouchers, conference/travel arrangements, supplies, office logs and letter files, along with many other secretarial functions. Created and implemented office guidelines and procedures.

<u>1981 - 1983. MOUNTAIN BELL. DENVER. STENOGRAPHER</u>

Worked in the Downtown Business Office maintaining customer account logs for 28 Service Representatives. Answered customer calls and directed them appropriately.

<u>1979 - 1981. MOUNTAIN BELL. DENVER. SECRETARY</u>

In the Comptrollers Department. Handled heavy typing of Bell System Practices for 8 computer programmers.

<u>1977 - 1979. MOUNTAIN BELL. DENVER. PROCESSING CLERK</u>

Processed statistical paper work for 7 Yellow Page Sales Representatives.

EDUCATION: Currently attending Denver College - W.P night classes.

TRAINING: Effective Writing - 1986. Vocabulary Study - 1984. Fortune Word-Fortune Electronic Mail - 1984. Effective Telephone/Communication Skills

PERSONAL:
- Volunteer work with Mountain Bell Telephone Pioneers
- Typing 90 W.P.M.
- Administrative Skills (efficient, good organizer, able to handle work systematically)
- Communication and telephone skills
- Self Starter - work independently to handle a variety of assignments
- Quick ability to learn the functions of any word processor

Executive Assistant

Jane Swift
9 Central Avenue
Chicago, IL 60625
(312) 555-1212

WORK EXPERIENCE

11/78 to Present — Custom Mouldings Inc., Chicago, IL

Office Coordinator/Assistant to V.P. of Operations
Responsibilities and duties include:

* Supervise and direct Secretary to Manufacturing Managers
* Compile and graph financial data and manufacturing information for weekly management meetings
* Process project support requests
* Maintain weekly project time sheets; summarize and initiate monthly intercompany and direct customer billings (data entry - IBM System/38)
* Graphics (presentations, forms, graphs, etc.)
* Typing and layout of bi-monthly company newsletter (Digital Word Processor)
* Routine secretarial functions; i.e., typing, assisting callers, maintaining confidentiality of salaries, proposed business plans, etc.
* Act as backup for Administrative Assistant to C.E.O.
* Employee Activities Committee member

7/73 to 11/78 — Plastic Products Ltd., Chicago, IL

Secretary to the Controller and Financial Planning Manager
Duties included:

* Data Entry (financial reports, budgets)
* Typed monthly and quarterly financial statements
* Assisted auditors with year-end audit
* Performed all day-to-day secretarial functions

EDUCATION

1971	Leominster High School Graduate (Business Course)
1980	C.M.E.A. Course - Basic Personnel Administration
1983	Calligraphy Course - Mount Wachusett Community College
1985	Introduction to Graphics course - Worcester Art Museum

OFFICE SKILLS — IBM System/38 user; IBM PC (Lotus/Symphony Software); Digital Word Processor; Dimension Switchboard; Dictaphone; IBM Typewriters. Typing 80 WPM.

REFERENCES — Furnished upon request

Fabric Salesperson

J A M E S S H A R P E, 9 Central Avenue, Kettering, OH 45429. (513) 555-1212

OBJECTIVE: A rewarding, challenging position that will capitalize on successful **SALES/MARKETING** and **MANAGEMENT** experience, and opportunities to initiate business strategies that will contribute to increased market penetration.

A C H I E V E M E N T S   A N D   Q U A L I F I C A T I O N S

* Built a strong retail dealer network from initial contact through training in sales, promotional, merchandising and pricing techniques with an emphasis on increasing territory revenues.
  — Increased wholesale revenues from $750,000 to $1.4 million.

* Prepared annual marketing objectives, operating budgets and forecasts.
  — Developed a marketing plan for a specific product, resulting in capture of 95% of the local market.

* Developed and implemented marketing plans specifically targeted to assigned territories and client type.
  — Moved employer to the dominant retailer position in its market by upgrading marketing/merchandising strategies.

* Tracked a variety of data to accurately forecast buying trends and motives as well as analyzing competitors, market positions, product lines and service levels.
  — Implemented assortment plans that increased gross profit margins from 40% to 51%.

* Monitored account follow-up activities resulting in increased client retention.
  — Successfully captured high-traffic/high-volume locations in over 60 department stores through supervision and implementation of extensive sales training to company merchandisers.

* Assembled complete proposals to include initial investment and cost justification.
  — Assisted in design of a UPC coding and POS plan to be utilized by store personnel in order to maintain more accurate inventories.

TRAVEL: Willing to travel extensively . . . Prefer relocation to the East Coast.

E X P E R I E N C E   H I G H L I G H T S

Dan River, New York, NY

KEY ACCOUNT MANAGER/MIDWEST. (1/85 - Present)

Control all sales, marketing and account servicing activities to all major department and specialty stores in Midwest with full profit and loss accountability. Assist clients for all in-store promotional events. Coordinate with client management for best product store positioning and display. Provide sales training seminars to client sales associates. Supervise merchandisers and inventory control personnel.

Walker Zanger, New York, NY

KEY ACCOUNTS REPRESENTATIVE/OHIO. (1/79-12/84)

Responsible for calling on all major department, specialty and mass merchandiser accounts in the Ohio and Kansas territory. Coordinated in-store promotional activities. Identified means to improve sales through advertising, merchandising and display methods. Increased revenues from $875,000 to $1.6 million.

Lenox China, Orland, FL

SALES REPRESENTATIVE/SOUTHEAST. (1/76 - 12/78)

Called on specialty and general merchandiser accounts in the Florida and southern Georgia area. Coordinated with client management to forecast market trends and identify which product lines would best improve client sales. Increased sales by 257%.

EDUCATION: B.A., City University of Chicago. Major - Marketing

---

STRENGTHS: I am competitive and innovative; with excellent communications and interpersonal skills. I possess accurate market forecasting abilities and am able to develop ideas into workable plans. Essentially profit-minded and results-oriented.

JAMES SHARPE, 9 Central Avenue, Arlington, MA 02174. (617) 555-1212.

QUALIFICATIONS SUMMARY

10 years of demonstrated sales experience drawing upon planning, persuasion, problem-solving and administration skills.

SELECTED ACHIEVEMENTS AND RESULTS

Planning
- Created and composed promotional materials for use with product line. Resulted in free product promotion in local and national publications. Valued at $650,000

- Presented, demonstrated, evaluated and published product information on a national basis. Resulted in increased expansion of distributor base and sales by 49%

Persuasion
- Influenced company management to expand product size through generated market research data and demonstrated product mix. Resulted in a 25% increase of total volume in each product.

- Persuaded organization to reduce sales territory and add personnel to form a first-time specialty products group. Resulted in increased awareness of product organizationally and within the industry.

Problem-Solving
- Resolved formulating equipment/product mismatch by designing new packaging. Resulted in increased sales of $250K.

- Identified high-use market for product and generated data to expand product usage. Resulted in increased sales of 70%.

Administration
- Co-directed the efforts of the marketing department through active participation on the corporate marketing board. Resulted in new advertising, package and product promotions.

- Synthesized intricate and diverse marketing training and product publication information. Resulted in increased market penetration.

WORK HISTORY

Regional Sales Representative, Phone Relays. Boston, MA.		77-Present
Sales Representative, Walsh Chemical. Worcester, MA.		1977
Retail Store Manager, Clothing Supply. Arlington, MA.		1974-1976
Assistant Dept. Manager, Penny's. Boston, MA.		1973-1974

EDUCATION
BA - Marketing, Columbia Pacific University, 1972.

Financial Executive Secretary

Jane Swift
9 Central Avenue
Nashville, TN 37211
(615) 555-1212

Employment History:

10/86 - Present

Commerce Bank & Trust Company, Nashville, TN
Executive Secretary
Secretary to two Vice Presidents of Commercial Loan. Duties included preparation of loan documents, processing of new funds, completion of computer input sheet for loan transactions, typing shorthand, and screening calls. Coordination and hostessing of a monthly breakfast meeting sponsored by the bank for area businesses. This involved mailing of invitations, taking reservations, making arrangements with the restaurant as well as hostessing the meeting.

Started as a Clerk/Typist in the Collection Department. After on year of employment was promoted to Secretary in Secured Lending Department. Held this position for 1 1/2 years at which time was promoted to above position as Executive Secretary in Commercial Loan Department.

7/83 - 10/86

The Nashville Bank, N.A. Nashville, TN
Executive Secretary
Secretary to Vice President Commercial Loan and Marketing. Duties include general secretarial (typing, shorthand, screening calls). Customer service for loan transactions and depository accounts. Responsible for advising all departments of new bank products and advertising of these products.

Education:

Nashville Community College
Secretarial Science (one semester)

Spencer Dynes High School
Business/Secretarial (graduated 1973 with honors)

References:

Furnished upon request.

Food and Beverage Service Director

Jane Swift
9 Central Avenue
Metairie, LA 70003
(504) 555-1212

A professional in the restaurant and resort business with a thorough background in the culinary service and accounting fields.

PRESENT: **METAIRIE TURF CLUB Metairie, Louisiana**
Food and Beverage Director

Directly responsible for start-up and management of all restaurant operations, group sales, central kitchen operations and purchasing.

The project hired 14 managers and 400 employees for a total Food & Beverage staff of $11,000,000. Formed the entire concession company in 3 months. Including: systems identification and implementation, hiring of staff, menus, table-top and uniform identification, training, product identification.

1977-86   **BRAUTIGANS Vail, Colorado**
Food and Beverage Manager

Hired as the Executive Chef and moved into the position of a Senior Food Services Manager overseeing 10 managers and over 150 employees in the area of conventions, commissary operations and purchasing for 14 restaurants.

Work Achievements: Restaurants served 25,000 quality meals per day. Successfully reduced the cost of sales consistently to 26% for the past three years on $8,000,000 gross revenue. Designed and implemented a new purchasing computer program including a recipe costing and inventory system.

1974-77   **KANCOLA CORPORATION Vail, Colorado**
Executive Chef

Executive Chef of the Cadillac Club and John Bull pub and restaurant.

ACTIVITIES: Involved in the Chef de Cuisine Association. Taught several classes connected with the Chef de Cuisine intern program, including a recent NIFDA course on sanitation.

Worked on the development and implementation of a two and six-week culinary seminar course with the National Culinary School.

EDUCATION: Culinary Institute of America

Food Product Manager

JANE SWIFT
9 CENTRAL AVENUE
AKRON, OH 44303
(216) 555-1212

EXPERIENCE
1970-Present

JUSTSO!, AKRON, OH
Manufacturer of cookies, crackers and snacks for the retail, food service and industrial markets.

1986-Present

GOVERNMENT PROGRAMS MANAGER, Food Service Division
Responsible for all governmental programs including Federal, State and Local. Directly involved in USDA Commodity Processing, Department of Defense, schools, military and elderly feeding programs. Administers and submits bids to government agencies, institutions and military service operations to achieve maximum sales and profit objectives. Supervises staff of four including government sales manager and customer service co-ordinators. Sales increase of 22%.

1984-1986

SENIOR PRODUCT MANAGER, Food Service Division
Developed new products outside traditional cookie/cracker markets via co-pack agreements. New Products now account for 15% of sales.

Responsibilities included market analysis, product development, co-packer search and development, manufacturing agreements and product introduction.

1983-1984

PRODUCT MANAGER, Food Service Division
Developed new products program, pricing, promotional and sales strategies. Introduced new vendor line of products, accounting for 8% of total division sales.

1981-1983

AREA MANAGER, Mid-West Food Service Division. Responsible for Chicago, Detroit, Columbus, Akron. Developed and maintained Regional level contacts with major national accounts. Implemented sales and marketing programs with staff of five territory managers and two sales representatives.

1978-1981

DISTRICT MANAGER, Food Service Division
Responsible for the Philadelphia and South Jersey Marketing Area.

1976-1978

DISTRICT MANAGER, Retail Division
Supervised eight direct salesmen and Assistant District Manager. Responsible for the Shop 'n Save, 7-11, and K-Mart chain accounts.

1974-1976

SALES TRAINER, Retail Division
Responsible for training all new salesmen in the Mid-West Sales Zone.

1970-74

SALESMAN, Retail Division
Responsible for sales to the Retail and Food Service Trade.

EDUCATION

B.A. Marketing 1976 (Ohio State University)

Food Service Salesperson

JAMES SHARPE
9 Central Avenue
Dayton, OH 45401
(513) 555-1212

OBJECTIVE

To secure a full-time marketing/management position offering personal growth, challenge, and responsibility.

EXPERIENCE

1984 to present

Food Service and Bakery Corporation, Dayton, OH.
Territory Manager
Responsibilities include administration of a territory encompassing all of Ohio and Michigan. Extensive contact with distributors selling premium brand and private label shortenings, oils, and margarines. Took on additional responsibility of the East Tennessee territory after one year. Responsibility for 55 million pounds of product with $1.2 million profit contribution.

1983 to 1984

FASTFOODS, Cincinnati, OH.
Territory Manager
Responsibilities included administration of a specified territory through contact with foodservice wholesale warehouse management and through operator contact on the end-user level. Account growth was achieved through sampling of products to qualified buyers, stressing features and benefits for specific menu applications, new product introductions, and effective promotions. Cited for Specialty New Account Sales.

1980 to 1983

KOSHER FOODS CORPORATION, New York, NY
Foodservice Division
Account Representative (1982 - 1983)
Sales Representative (1980 - 1982)
Salesman of the Year 1983. Runner-up, 1982

EDUCATION

Columbia University, New York, NY. B.B.A. - Marketing, 1980.

AFFILIATIONS

American Marketing Association

Health Care Professional

Jane Swift
9 Central Avenue
Seattle, WA 98102
(206) 555-1212

OBJECTIVE

Management/Marketing position in Health Care setting.

SUMMARY

Experienced Health Care professional with working knowledge of home health inhospital-based and free standing agencies in addition to promotion of retail sales of medical equipment and services.

EXPERIENCE

1987	**Home Care Inc., Seattle, WA**

Responsible for development and implementation of a total scope, home IV therapy program. Includes home total parenteral nutrition in accordance with NITA standards. Performed budgetary control duties and ensured organizational proficiency and compliance with all State and Federal regulations.
Additional responsibilities include: Sales, marketing and purchasing for eleven durable medical equipment outlets.

1983-87   **Seattle General Hospital, Seattle, WA**

Progressive positions in the Home Care Department reaching the position of Home Care Coordinator for the City Hospital District. As Department Head, held responsibility for scheduling, planning and supervision of 15 professional and numerous non-professional workers.

Developed community awareness and doubled the amount of services provided to the community in the area of home health care.

EDUCATION

1982   **Registered Nursing Degree, Columbia Basin College (Pasco, WA)**

Health Care Sales Manager

JAMES SHARPE
9 Central Avenue
Indianapolis, IN 46206
(317) 555-1212

SUMMARY:
Extensive experience managing a sales function selling directly and through brokers. Strong background in implementing sales techniques through training, motivation, and effective sales meetings.

BUSINESS
EXPERIENCE:
A Pharmacueticals Manufacturer. Consumer Healthcare Division. District Sales Manager (1980 to Present)

Responsible for sales and profit objectives. Responsible for broker test program, broker selection, and broker management.

Recruit, train and direct five Key Account Representatives and three Merchandisers.

Accomplishments:

* During my tenure, nine new products have been introduced and sales volume has climbed from $2.1 million to $7.3 million.

* Converted strong business relationships with retail customers into new broker business.

* Attained 14-21% sales increase through broker management in two years.

* District Manager of the Year for five of the last eight years

* Second-highest Unit manager in 1987 with attainment of + 137% of budget.

Key Account Representative (1978 to 1980)

Responsible for the sales, distribution and promotion of health care products to all classes of trade in Midwest. My territory contributed 28% of the district's volume.

Successfully introduced three new products and attained a 37% increase in sales my last full year in the territory.

MEAD JOHNSON, Sales Representative (1973-1978)

Responsible for the sales, distribution and promotion of Carter products to all classes of trade in West Texas.

Increased territory volume 31% in two years. Successfully introduced five new products.

EDUCATION:
1972, Princeton University. Major: Marketing

SEMINARS:
Master Salesmanship Course - Clement Communications
Various other salesmanship and managerial courses

AFFILIATION:
American Marketing Association

REFERENCES:
References will be furnished upon request.

High Tech Sales Manager

Jane Swift
9 Central Avenue
Dallas, TX 75231
(214) 555-1212

Education: George Washington University, BBA: 1964

Position Desired: Financially and professionally rewarding sales management/sales position in the Southeastern United States.

PROFESSIONAL HISTORY

1986 - Present

Company: Compugraphic

Position: District Sales Manager

Territory: Southeastern United States

Accomplishments: Successful sales/sales management, account management and installation supervision of all systems integration network products offered by Compugraphic Company.

1983 - 1986

Company: Teletone Corporation

Position: Area Sales Manager/Regional Rep. Sales Manager

Territory: Southeastern United States

Accomplishments: Sold and managed successfully in Southeastern region.
Customer base generated, consisting of both private industry and government accounts. During my tenure, region remained at over, or near, assigned quotas consistently.

Products: 1. All D.O.V. products
2. Time division and statistical multiplexes

NOTE: Acquired good working knowledge of P.B.X. and call distribution markets in area of telephony.

1981 - 1983

Company: Four Phase Systems, Inc.

Position: Major Account Representative

Territory: Georgia and Alabama (selected areas)

Accomplishments: Developed many major accounts to the level of national account status. Sample accounts: Coca-Cola International, Revere Copper & Brass, Rust Engineering, Jim Walters Corp., Equifax and others.

Presidents Club two years. In 1982 ranked sixth of 127 sales representatives.

1978 - 1981

Company:	Control Data Corporation
Position:	Major Account Rep (Nuclear Specialist)
Territory:	Georgia, Alabama, Mississippi
Accomplishments:	Sold successfully all Cybernet products to wide variety of customers with particular emphasis on electronics design and manufacturing and nuclear applications. Sample accounts: Georgia Power, Gulf Power, Mississippi Power & Light, U.S. Army Corps of Engineers (Vicksburg, MS), Scientific Atlanta.

1974 - 1978

Company:	General Electric Corporation
Position·	National Account Manager, Branch Manager
Territory·	Long Island, New York
Accomplishments:	National Account Manager for Cooper & Lybrand. Promoted to Branch Manager, Long Island Branch. During tenure as Branch Manager my territorial responsibility slightly more than tripled the monthly revenue generated from previous monthly averages.

1969 - 1974

Company:	Mohawk Data Science
Position:	Sales Representative
Territory:	New York City
Accomplishments:	Sold successfully all M.D.S. offerings, source data, communications and ancillary products.

1965 - 1969

Company·	Control Data Corporation
Position·	Sales Representative
Territory:	Washington, DC (government and commercial)
Accomplishments:	Sales trainee (18 months). Sold and installed systems in U.S. Department of Agriculture, U.S. Department of Health, Education and Welfare, Internal Revenue Service, People's Drug Stores, Inc. and Marriott Corporation.

SUMMATION:

My twenty-two years of experience in the data processing world have provided me with a knowledge of source data automation, half/full duplex communications, large mainframe systems, optical character recognition equipment, medium to small computer systems, scientific and general business application software packages, local area networking data over voice products, data switching systems, P.B.X., A.C.D. and related telephony equipment, as well as trained and implemented sales and managerial skills.

- References will be furnished upon request -

High-Tech Salesperson

Jane Swift
9 Central Avenue
Boston, MA 02127
(617) 555-1212

POSITION DESIRED:
Professionally rewarding sales position that will offer an opportunity for professional growth and advancement based upon a demonstrated strength in opening new accounts.

EXPERIENCE

1987
to
present

Marketing Representative. Major Computer Manufacturer.
Marketed large mainframe CPU, disk drives and tape drives. Quota: $2.5M. Competition: IBM.
Accomplishments:
Sales: $2.6 million
Opened Chevron Account with CPU, July 1987
Opened Bell Southwestern Services account, October 1987

1984
to
1987

Account Manager. Storage Technology Corporation.
Marketed disk drives, tape drives and memory for CPU's printers and professional service packages to the Fortune 500 companies. Competition: IBM.
Accomplishments:
Sales: $4.5 million
Helped open Southwestern Bell
Earned Corporate Club in 1982 and 1983
National recognition for first firm order of new product

1980
to
1984

Marketing Representative. Control Data.
Marketed disk drives, tape drives and printers.
Competition IBM. Responsible for four new accounts and three add-on orders with existing accounts. Quota: $1.7M.
Accomplishments:
Sales: $2.3 million
#1 salesman in nation in 1984, 1982.
#2 salesman in nation in 1983

EDUCATION
George Washington University, BBA; 1978

SUMMARY
My experience in the data processing world have provided me with a knowledge of large, medium and small computer systems, and general business application software packages. My track record proves my belief that every objection brings you closer to the sale.

Hospital Pharmacist

James Sharpe, 9 Central Avenue, Clifton, NJ 07013. (201) 555-1212

OBJECTIVES:

To use my pharmacy, communication, administrative, and organizational skills in a challenging position as a hospital pharmacist.

EXPERIENCE:

Resident Pharmacist. *Teaneck Community Hospital. May 1986 - Present*
Pharmacy administration, provision of drug information/poison control center services, clinical services, outpatient pharmacy services, and investigational drug services.
Duties included rotations throughout all areas of a progressive, computerized hospital pharmacy department. Including: Drug Information, Medical Information, Administration, Clinical Pharmacy, Outpatient Pharmacy, and Investigational Drug Services

Staff Pharmacist, *Centralized and Decentralized Services. Mahwah Cottage Hospital. May 1983 - May 1986*
Inpatient unit dose drug distribution and IV admixutre services; participation in daily hematology and GI patient rounds; discharge patient counseling. Provision of drug information to hospital staff; participation on aminoglyoside pharmacokinetic monitoring service; training and education of new pharmacists and pharmacy students.

Pharmacy Extern. *Mahwah Cottage Hospital. February 1983 - May 1983*
IV admixture preparation, unit dose drug distribution, maintenance of patient profiles, and quality assurance procedures.

Pharmacy Extern. *Apothecary. Mahwah Cottage Hospital. November 1982 - February 1983*
Participated in patient counseling, patient profile maintenance, extensive extemporaneous compounding service, and inventory control.

APPOINTMENTS:

American Hospital Formulary Service Reviewer

REGISTRATION:

State of New Jersey

AFFILIATIONS:

American Society of Hospital Pharmacists
American Pharmaceutical Association
American Society of Hospital Pharmacists

EDUCATION:

Bachelor of Science, Pharmacy, New Jersey Institute of Technology 1983

Inventory Control Buyer

Jane Swift
9 Central Avenue
San Francisco, CA 94123
(415) 555-1212

PROFILE:
Results-oriented Manager, verse in total project implementation and staff development. Expertise in creating highly expeditious systems and procedures maximizing efficiency and minimizing time consumption. Extensive troubleshooting experience.

PROFESSIONAL EXPERIENCE:

I. MAGNIN, San Francisco, CA. 1981 - Present.

Inventory Control Buyer: 1/83 - Present

As inventory control buyer for I. Magnin's catalogue division:

* Increased net shipping, resulting in **6%** sales beyond initial projection.

* Trained retail buyers in direct mail buying techniques and catalogue fulfillment, increasing divisional net sales **12%** and maximizing staff management potential.

* Created unique systems and procedures which increased production efficiency by **15%.**

* Controlled flow of merchandise to maximize net shipping and minimize markdowns.

Direct Mail Coordinator: 11/81 - 1/83

* Initiated catalogue production schedule. Supervised projects with emphasis on copy and merchandise management. Maintained in-house production schedules.

MATHEW BENDER (Scientific Publications) New York, NY. Editor 7/79 - 10/81

* Initiated, supervised and reviewed all production phases for four journals. Controlled quality of copy editing and art mechanicals. Pre- and post verification of the printing process. Approved promotion copy.

EDUCATION: BA: Communications. Hofstra University, 1979

Junior Accounting Clerk

James Sharpe
9 Central Avenue
Huntington Beach, CA 92649
(714) 555-1212

OBJECTIVE: A challenging position in the accounting profession

WORK EXPERIENCE:
June 1986 - January 1987   HUNTINGTON BEACH GAZETTE
                                  Huntington Beach, CA

                                  Accounting Clerk for classified accounting. Duties
                                  included accounts receivable on Vax system, balanc-
                                  ing, adjusting, and posting receivables. Heavy phone
                                  contact with customers for collections. Collections
                                  improved 7%.

March 1986 - June 1986   AIN ASSOCIATES
                                  Los Angeles, CA

                                  General office work for temporary employment agency.
                                  Duties included clerk in Tax office, clerk in Health
                                  Insurance Company, and A/R for construction company.

August 1985 - March 1986   CALA FOODS
                                  Los Angeles, CA

                                  Cashier. Worked independently doing all cashier duties,
                                  some bookkeeping and inventory.

EDUCATION
March 1986 - March 1987   CALIFORNIA SCHOOL OF ACCOUNTING
                                  Los Angeles, CA

                                  Graduate in March of 1987 with a certificate as a
                                  Computer Accounting Assistant. Courses include
                                  Accounting, Business Math, Basic Programming,
                                  Integrated Accounting on IBM PC and Lotus. Plan on
                                  continuing with night courses for degree.

REFERENCES   Personal references available upon request.

Law Clerk

Jane Swift
9 Central Ave.
Downers Grove, IL 60515
(312) 555-1212

Objective: To obtain a position in which I can utilize my work experience and education.

EMPLOYMENT

1987 - Present   United States Court of Appeals. Second Circuit, Chicago, IL
INFORMATION CLERK

Answer procedural questions regarding local rules and Federal Rules of Appellate Procedures. Respond to inquiries from a wide range of sources including the media, attorneys and litigants. Receive and review over-the-counter filings such as briefs, motions, appendices, and petitions for rehearing for format, time constraints, and proof of service.

1984-1987   United States District Court. Southern District, Chicago, IL
PRO SE WRIT CLERK

Answer procedural questions regarding local rules. Examine all complaints to determine if they are in proper form for filing. Ensure petitioners and complainants understand procedural requirements. Maintain liaison with State Attorney General's staff, state prison authorities and other agencies concerning prisonere complaints and petitions. Prepare statistical reports and analyses of pending matters.

1981 - 1984   Department of Justice. U.S. Attorney's Office. Southern District of Chicago.
LEGAL CLERK

Research of documents and inquiries for individual Assistant U.S. Attorneys. Issue warrants for arrest; process writs of habeas corpues, AD testificandum prosequendum; verify prison surrenders. Record Keeping of criminal calendars, processing of legal documents, up-dating computer.

EDUCATION   City University of Chicago. B.A. 1980. Major: Business Management

References furnished upon request.

Lease Accountant

James Sharpe
9 Central Avenue
Englewood, NJ 07632
(201) 555-1212

OBJECTIVE: Pursuing a career position which requires a motivated, dedicated, above-average person, and where individual achievements and performance will be recognized, thereby allowing opportunities for growth and development.

EXPERIENCE:

8/84-Present   Lease Accountant, Trump Financial Corp. NY.
Duties include maintaining general ledger, preparation of journal vouchers, bank reconciliations, financial statements, taxes, monthly account analyses, and customer service.

Administrative Coordinator
Ensured compliance with departmental monthly activity reporting procedures. Maintained a central control for all purchase requisitions and reviewed departmental billings, both inward and outward.

11/81-08/84   Administrative Assistant, Citibank, NY.
Assisted in developing annual revenue forecasts, automating the planning function on various Personal Computers to generate timely reports for management. Corresponded with lessees regarding billings and accounts receivable.

OTHER DATA: Skilled in the use of IBM PC-LOTUS 1-2-3, Data General, IBM Displaywriter, Logicalc, IBM CRT, Apple MAC II, Dynoplan, TSO, and SPF.

EDUCATION: MBA with concentration in Finance, Columbia University
B.S. Degree, majored in Business Administration.

REFERENCES: Will be furnished upon request.

Legal Office Manager

James Sharpe
9 Central Avenue
Raleigh, NC 27612

EXPERIENCE

9/83 to Present

Glick & Gregory, Raleigh, NC

Office Manager for general practice law firm. The firm has 40 attorneys and 50 support staff.

Achievements

*Provided direction and supervision for support staff. Recruited, interviewed and hired support personnel. Conducted annual performance reviews and recommended salary and bonus increases for staff. Developed office manual with general policies and procedures for the firm.

*Evaluated and recommended word processing and data processing equipment. Created word processing center to best meet the demands of the firm. Participated in the conversion of manual accounting system to an in-house IBM-36 System.

*Planned and executed major installation of telephone equipment. Instituted long distance discount service to reduce cost of long distance calls. Established a central message center to alleviate demands on the main board.

*Established an alpha/numerical filing system which provided a standard format and resulted in a decrease in lost or misfiled files.

*Administered insurance benefits for the firm and its employees. Reviewed insurance policies to keep premiums within reason and insurance coverage at appropriate levels.

2/79 to 9/83

Law Office of Richard Kiley Esq, Raleigh, NC

Assistant Office Manager with responsibility for petty cash for office, filing, inventory, and ordering of supplies; bookkeeping for special clients, travel arrangements.

*Instituted automated W.P for the firm;

EDUCATION: Fordham University

REFERENCES: Available upon request.

Legal Secretary

Jane Swift
9 Central Avenue
Billings, Mt 59104
(406) 555-1212

OBJECTIVE:

Seeks responsible position that will utilize my diversified experience.

WORK EXPERIENCE:

John Courtis & Partners - 1985-Present
Legal Secretary to Senior Managing Partner
Administrative responsibilities extending to preparation of highly confidential/sensitive legal documentation and correspondence; mergers and acquisitions, litigation, criminal. Interviewing/testing/hiring/training/supervision of non-management level support staff.

Duveen, Eal & Gold - 1982-1985
Office Administrator/Executive Assistant to Senior Managing Partner
Interviewing/hiring of non-management level support staff; monitored financial investment portfolio; preparation and production of correspondence and financial information for lending institutions and clients; heavy client contact and coordination of appointment calendar. Assisted in preparation of annual budget.

Capital Management Corporation - 1979-1982
Office Manager/Executive Assistant to CEO
Responsible for all phases off start-up operation; preliminary contract negotiations with electricians, carpenters, maintenance staff, telephone installers. Researched and evaluated all equipment requirements, purchased all office furniture and supplies. Extensive travel arrangements; year-end compilation of all tax filing information; maintained corporate bank accounts up through bank reconciliation.

Bays Discount Stores - 1977-1979
Office Administrator/Executive Assistant to President
Developed and monitored an effective customer service program; instrumental in incorporation of same in overall training program; liaison for management staff and executive committee.

EDUCATION:

B.A., Psychology, Minor: Economics - Fordham University
Further Graduate Studies - New York University
Notary Public for State of New York
Licensed Insurance Agent - State of New York

Major Account Executive

James Sharpe, 9 Central Avenue, Glendale, CA 91209. (818)555-1212

OBJECTIVE

Sales management position using expertise in motivating sales personnel, increasing sales and creation of effective programs contributing to higher organizational profits and market share.

WORK HISTORY

HEADQUARTERS ACCOUNT MANAGER
Major Food Co., Consumer Products Group. Glendale, CA. October 1986 – Present
National account management of a two-million-dollar account. Responsible for staff of fourteen, covering five states. Responsibilities include formulating profit structure, constructing and formulating all promotional activities, setting up all co-op advertising, feature pricing, establishing goals, organizing inventory control of spoils and damages.

*Doubled promotional activity, which has increased sales by 12% and profits by 6%.
*Reinstated extender and merchandising program, increasing sales by over twenty thousand dollars per month.

SALES REPRESENTATIVE
Grocery Products Division. May 1983 – October 1986

Serviced territory consisting of Northern and Southern California; concentration on independent and chain accounts. Complete control of service, sales and in-store promotional activity.

*Increased client base through prospecting by 28% or eight new accounts, for a total of 1.9 million in increased sales.

SALES REPRESENTATIVE
Durkee, Inc., Institutional Sales Division. Cleveland, OH. December 1980 – May 1983
Responsible for horizontal and vertical sales growth of full line food service products to accounts within a defined territory.
*Doubled sales volume and profit margin within first year. #2 salesperson in region.
*Voluntarily relinquished territory to establish new territory in unsold area. Within six months built sales to match original territory.

MANAGER
Cheers Restaurant, Boston MA. June 1978 – December 1980
Responsible for 20 employees. Duties included: bookkeeping, pricing, ordering and product inventory control. Food planning, preparation and a daily schedule. Implemented time study for daily operations.
*Reduced expenses and overhead by 20%.
*Maintained a 40% net profit.
*Increased business by 33%.

EDUCATION

Georgetown University (Washington, DC). B.S. Degree: Planning and Administration
*Graduated with honors

Manufacturing Systems Engineer

James Sharpe
9 Central Avenue
WARREN, MI 48090
(313) 555-1212

SUMMARY:

A seasoned Manufacturing Engineer, with strong developmental skills and realtime experience. Extensive work with Cobol, alc and pascal. New development work with Burroughs B7900 and A10

WORK HISTORY:

1984 to Present   **MANUFACTURING SYSTEMS ENGINEER, AMC, DETROIT, MI.**

Assignments include:
* Programming major enhancements to realtime systems.
* System support of current and new systems through transition period.
* Extensive system use of TPS and DMS technology.
* Rewriting batch system for Receiving Inspection function.
* Extensive customer interface and user training.

1982 to 1984   **INVENTORY SYSTEM CLERK, State University of California at Davis.**

Assignments included:
* Computer and word processing input.
* Computer maintenance reports.
* Updating computer inventories.
* Tracking of excess/surplus university equipment.

EDUCATION & TRAINING:

Bachelor of Science in Business Administration - 5/82.
State University of CA at Davis. Concentrations in Finance and Computer Systems.

Professional Workshops:

EDS - System Engineer Development Program
DMS II
Burroughs Workflow Language

REFERENCES: References will be forwarded upon request.

Marketing Analyst

JANE SMITH
9 Central Avenue
DEARBORN, MI 48126
(313) 555-1212

EXPERIENCE

Daytons, Inc. (Detroit, MI)   July 1985 to Present
MARKETING ANALYST - Provide a broad-based flow of data for merchandisers,
buyers, Catalog Distribution Center associates and management to assure
continuing high-level profitability of the company's catalog sales. Access all
databases by CRT terminal using CRIMS, on-line system interfacing with ISA,
IDB, MIDB, Computer Analyses focus on:
o Historical applications, such as impact of season, media ads, space, price
   and color changes
o Reliable pre-season forecasts of catalog demand patterns and
   in-season revisions where necessary to maintain inventory control
o Study of inventory turnover in relation to buying estimates, commitments
   and quality of merchandise
o Choice of models and development of new ones for item estimating
o Identification of systems problems in estimates above or below plan
o Establishment of recommendations for inventory surplus solutions
o Decision-marketing, planning, scheduling to meet data deadlines

Zachary & Front Advertising, Inc.   New York, NY Summer 1984
OFFICE MANAGER - Arranged for in-house weekly newsletter and biweekly
policy memos for new agency. Developed billing system, dealt with clients and
managed clerical staffing.

Tisch Properties New York,   NY Winter 1984
ASSISTANT BOOKKEEPER - Worked with accounts receivable payable, bank
Reconciliations.

EDUCATION
State University of Ohio
B.S., Business Administration, 1985
Concentration: Marketing and Management Information Systems

COMPUTER SKILLS: BASIC, COBOL, FCS-EPS, and SPSS software package

References Available Upon Request

Mechanical Engineer

James Sharpe
9 Central Avenue
MORRISTOWN, NJ 07869
(201) 555-1212

OBJECTIVE
Seek employment as a design or project engineer with the opportunity for continued professional growth

WORK EXPERIENCE

1984 to Present - Project Engineer. Purdue Farms.

Responsible for project management during construction of a 600-ton feed receiving, storage, blending, and load-out facility. Design implementation and testing of heating/ventilation system for poultry grow-out houses. System design and cost estimate on complete system for caged grow-out.

1981 to 1984 - Project Engineer. R.T French Co.

Responsibilities included design and installation of an electronically controlled in-plant bulk caustic distribution system. Major repairs to a large multi-cell cooling tower and two evaporators. Feasibility study and cost estimate for 70,000 square foot dock-high warehouse development for renovating 1/4 mile of rail spur.

1978 to 1981 - Production Engineer Reckitt & Coleman Co

Responsible for machine and system design, production scheduling, procurement scheduling and quality control, for walnut processing. Redesign of conveyors and elevators reduced manufacturing labor simplified maintenance and improved quality. Instituted a system of material control to account for all materials used.

EDUCATION
University of California, Davis, CA. M.S. in Engineering/Agricultural Engineering—1978.
B.S. in Agricultural Engineering—1976.

PROFESSIONAL ORGANIZATIONS
American Society of Agricultural Engineers
American Welding Society

REFERENCES AVAILABLE UPON REQUEST

Medical Equipment Salesperson

JAMES SHARPE

9 Central Avenue
New Hope, MN 55428
(612)555-1212

CAREER OBJECTIVE:
To become the top salesperson in a progressive company with quality products.

CAREER DEVELOPMENT

1980 to Present — Sales Representative
LIFE MEDICAL EQUIPMENT CO., Los Angeles, CA
Sales to doctors, hospitals and distributors throughout Minnesota.
Established a strong dealer network of 25+ since 1980.
Increased Total Sales Volume from $15,000 (1980) to $800,000 (1987).
Top salesperson in region for last 5 years.
In top 5% of sales nationwide: 1985, 1986, 1987.

1978 - 1980 — District Manager
UNIFORMS R US, Boston, MA
Sold uniforms, patches and business clothing to industrial and commercial accounts in New England.
Exceeded sales objectives by an average of 32% each year.

1975 - 1978 — Sales Representative
HOSPITAL SUPPLY, Memphis, TN
Sold textiles, uniforms, draperies, furniture and equipment to hospitals and nursing homes.
Established sales and developed a territory that had no previous sales representation in TN.
Total sales over $300,000 a year.

1969 - 1975 — Sales Representative
BAYOU SURGICAL SUPPLY, New Orleans, LA
Sold surgical and hospital supplies to doctors, hospitals and nursing homes. Established sales in a territory with no previous sales representation with a new company.
Increased sales from $100,000 a year in first to $400,000 in later years.

EDUCATION: B.A. - Political Science (Tulane University, New Orleans, LA)

PERSONAL: Single, Excellent health, willing to travel & relocate.

REFERENCES: Available upon request.

Medical Goods Sales Manager

JAMES SHARPE, 9 Central Avenue, SYRACUSE, NY 13217. (315) 555-1212

OBJECTIVE   To continue expansion of business acumen, experience, judgment and responsibility. To be compensated on achievements and have opportunity to work in challenging environment.

WORK EXPERIENCE

Present   **SALES MANAGER, S.W. REGION, for Pharmaceutical Co.**
Provided training, leadership, and decision-making responsibilities to expand the marketing efforts of the S.W. Region.
Contributed $3.2 million in revenues on budgeted operating expenses of $8555,000
Directed a sales force of 4 and an operational support staff of 15 people.

1984-1986   **SENIOR SALES CONSULTANT/NATIONAL ACCOUNT COORDINATOR**
Coordinated American Medical International Account which contributed 1.2 million for 98 hospitals.
Managed a territory which generated 1.7 million in 1985.
Responsible for marketing revenues in Texas, Oklahoma, Louisiana, and Arkansas.

1982-1984   **SENIOR SALES REPRESENTATIVE, Mead Johnson, Chicago, IL**
Attained Sr. Sales Representative position, one of nine in corporate sales force of 133.
Managed territory which represented 1.3 million in total revenues for 1984.
Contributed $550,000 in new account revenues, by duration, for 1984.

1979-1982   **SALES REPRESENTATIVE, Whitehall Labs, Syracuse, NY**
Responsible for marketing coverage for three branch offices in two states, Texas and New Mexico, for all market types.
Attained New Sales Leader for S.W. Region in 1st, 2nd, and 4th quarters for 1981.
Provided Whitehall with excess of $300,000 in new account revenues, for 1982.
Managed territory which represents $1.1 million in total revenues for 1982.

EDUCATION   **TEXAS A & M:** B.A., 1979. Major-Biology; Minor-Chemistry

Microcomputer Support Analyst

Jane Swift, 9 Central Avenue, San Antonio, TX 78230. (512) 555-1212

Hardware: IBM Personal Computer, Compaq, Displaywriter System; NEC Personal Computer; Facet Plotter (HP7478); Epson FX Printers; Xerox Memory-writer (627 & 630).

Software: BASIC, DOS, Data Base III, Lotus 1-2-3, Nutshell, Smart-Key, Multi-Mate

EXPERIENCE:

A SAN ANTONIO TECHNICAL SERVICES COMPANY (JANUARY '84-PRESENT)
MICROCOMPUTER SUPPORT ANALYST
* Provide Lotus 1-2-3 & Nutshell data base management consultation and data entry services
* Lotus 1-2-3 Experience:
- Create data base file & guidelines for over 950 drawings
- Compile weekly Itinerary Report
- Prepare graphics presentation material
* IBM PC Experience:
- Configure software for system compatibility
- Compile programs into Machine Language
- Respond to device error messages
- Provide system maintenance tasks
* Co-ordinate organization of technical proposals under deadline:
- Facilitate conversion of IBM 5520 system disks to CPR series 8500
* On-the-spot decision making & problem solving responsibilities to facilitate disk conversion.

1ST DALLAS BANK (JUNE '82-JANUARY '84) EVALUATION SUPERVISOR
* Responsible for the overall supervision, evaluation & implementation of quality control procedures and personnel
* Trained new employees on program guidelines
* Assisted evaluators in implementation of program
* Reviewed all employee evaluations
* Contracted with employment agencies to hire temporary help

AUSTIN SCHOOL FOR THE DEAF (SEPTEMBER '81-JANUARY '82)
COUNSELOR
* Planned & implemented living skills & leisure activities for developmentally disabled & emotionally disturbed residential students
* Established procedures for integrating clients into residential social functions
* Developed new community contacts and services

EDUCATION:

Computer Applications in Business, North Shore Community College, Bekerley, MA (June '83)

BA Sociology, Westmont College, Santa Barbara, CA (June '80)

REFERENCES:

Upon Request

Jane Swift
9 Central Avenue
Chicago, IL 60654
(312) 555-1212

PROFESSIONAL
GOALS   Integrating care in a neonatal nursery as a Clinical
                 Specialist involving the clinical support of infants and
                 children.

EDUCATION
  1988   Master of Science in Nursing from the University of
                 Illinois. This degree is a Clinical Specialty in Pediatrics
                 with a minor in Education. The pediatric focus is
                 neonatology.

  1985   Bachelor of Science in Nursing. Graduated with honors.

EXPERIENCE

                 Methodist Conference Center. Chicago (1988, Summer)
                 Position: Media Specialist
                 -Created and executed special media presentations for the
                  National Senior High Youth Conferences.
                 -Coordinated all media utilized during the conference,
                  working with other conference leadership.

                 The University of Illinois Medical School (August 1987-May
                 1988)
                 Position: Graduate Assistant
                 -Worked in association with graduate faculty in planning
                  and designing research studies.
                 -Performed literature searches and review for research
                  studies, presentations, and journal writings.
                 -Consolidated data for reports.
                 -Executed telephone interviews for data gathering.

                 Children's Hospital, Chicago (October 1985-December 1986)
                 Position: Staff nurse in the neonatal intensive care unit.

AFFILIATIONS

                 Illinois Nurses Association
                 National Association of Neonatal Nurses
                 Association of Critical-Care Nurses

REFERENCES   Available upon request.

Occupational Therapist

JAMES SHARPE
9 CENTRAL AVENUE
ATLANTA, GA 30305
(404) 555-1212

Employment

3/84-Present	**Occupational Therapy Department** **St Joseph's Hospital, Atlanta, GA** **Staff Occupational Therapist, Registered/Licensed**
1/82-3/84	**Occupational Therapy Department, Baylor Medical Center, Dallas, TX** **Staff Occupational Therapist**
1/79-1/82	**Occupational Therapy Department, Kaiser Medical Center, San Francisco, CA** **Occupational Therapy Assistant**

Education

University of Georgia. Graduated 1979
Degree: Bachelor of Science in Occupational Therapy
Cumulative GPA: 3.8   Major GPA: 3.93

Special Projects:

Private Practice: Pediatrics. Independent Study: Child Life Program; Play Therapy

Fieldworks:

Physical Dysfunction. Psycho-Social. Pediatrics

Affiliations

American Occupational Therapy Association (AOTA)
Georgia Occupational Therapy Association (GOTA)

Personal

Excellent health, no physical limitations. Will relocate.

Reference List Available Upon Request

Office Administrator

James Sharpe
9 Central Avenue
Columbus, OH 43232
(614) 555-1212

OBJECTIVE   To obtain a responsible and challenging position in the business field where my educational and work experience would have valuable application.

EXPERIENCE   OHIO WHOLESALE DRUG CO., COLUMBUS, OH. OCTOBER 1979-PRESENT.
*Manage correspondence and all travel arrangements and accommodations for Executives.

*Meeting Planner for annual Trade Show.

*Handle billing of special orders for entire chain, plus Coupon Redemption Program

*Responsible for all personnel records and payroll, Workman's Compensation Forms and insurance claims.

PLAINS STATE COMPANY, COLUMBUS, OH. 1976 - 1979.
EXECUTIVE SECRETARY

*Responsible for outgoing and incoming mail, inventory control, correspondence for late notices and reminders to overdue accounts, collection of salesman monies and also the posting, and cash application to these accounts,

*Processed orders, correspondence of all office Executives.

*Handled payroll, including salesman commissions, ordering of all office supplies, extensive telephone contact.

EDUCATION   Columbus Community College. Graduated May 1976, Dean's List, major course of study and concentration in Medical Secretary Procedures.

SKILLS   Typing: 95 W.P.M   Shorthand: 100 W.P.M.

REFERENCES   Furnished upon request

Office Manager

Jane Swift
9 Central Avenue
Los Angeles, CA 90071
(213) 555-1212

EXPERIENCE: Office Manager, Buy Rite Liquors.
                Wholesaler of alcoholic beverages
                May 1979 - present

Began as a bookkeeper, became Office Manager in 1983. Set up and maintain all billings and accounts receivable files. Set up and maintenance of payroll. Monthly, quarterly, and annual reports to Federal and State agencies. Obtain and maintain listing of fleet of trucks and automobiles for registration and insurance.

* Reorganized the accounting system and instituted a 'one-write' system. Time reduction of an estimated 36 hours per working week.

* Supervised the transfer of accounting procedures to a Digital Mini-computer in January, 1977, updated to a PDP-1134 in October, 1980. Presently implementing an Accounts Payable System. Reduced staff from five to three, or 40% office payroll reduction.

* Created and maintained an electronic tracking system for delivery schedules and driver availability. Increased on-time deliveries 10% off-peak, 14% peak traffic times (such as Christmas). Substantially increased sales volume.

EDUCATION: Los Angeles Community College
                Accounting Courses, 1973 - 1975   3.5 CUM GPA

REFERENCES: Given upon request.

Operating Room Services Specialist

Jane Swift
9 Central Avenue
Madison,WI 53708
(608) 555-1212

OBJECTIVE:

Management Position: An opportunity in management to demonstrate how my skills and experience can improve operations.

PROFESSIONAL HISTORY:

St. Cecilia Hospital, Madison, WI. 1983 to Present

Director of Operating Room Services. Includes Operating Room, Post-Anesthesia Care Unit, Anesthesia, and Ambulatory Surgery.

Management of 110 employees
Develop departmental goals and objectives, and establish and maintain departmental budgets.

Significant Accomplishments

◊ Planned and oversaw renovation of 16 Operating Room Suites;

◊ Developed team concept and clinical ladder;

◊ Established operating room preceptorship;

◊ Instituted block scheduling;

◊ Developed quality assurance program for departments.

Sister of Charity, Sebastopol, CA. 1977-1983

Assistant Service Supervisor, General Surgery. Maintained efficient unit activities. Assisted in training and education of service personnel. Assisted with employee performance appraisals. Requisitioned supplies and equipment.

Operating Room Specialist, Cardiovascular. 1975-1977. Planned, implemented, and evaluated patient care intraoperatively. Selected and prepared supplies and equipment. Assumed roles of scrub and circulating nurse.

Operating Room Nurse Intern. 1974-1975. Learned to function in the roles of scrub and circulating nurse

EDUCATION:

University of Alabama, Birmingham
1974, BSN

Supervisory Management Course: American Management Association

Operations Management Specialist

OBJECTIVE

A position within the operations management environment.

SUMMARY OF QUALIFICATIONS

SALES/MARKETING

◇ Successful sales and marketing background.
◇ Adept with vendor/manufacturer representation.
◇ Direct customer/vendor contact, including consumer and warranty resolution.
◇ Capable of presentations; acquisition, finance and legal formats.
◇ Demonstrated ability with promotional/merchandising design, planning, and implementation.
◇ Colorado Real Estate Sales License.

ADMINISTRATION MANAGEMENT

◇ Knowledgeable of design and construction practices.
◇ Construction coordination of "turn-key" multi/single housing units.
◇ Proficient with consumer real estate financing, including correspondent banking techniques.
◇ Practiced with work scheduling (equipment and personnel), contractor coordination, site inspection and representation to municipalities.
◇ Accustomed to working on tight deadlines.
◇ Knowledgeable of supervision and training procedures.
◇ Experienced with corporate start-up administration.

TECHNICAL

◇ Superior written and verbal communication skills, technical writing, blueprints and site plans.
◇ Conducted detailed site and completion inspections.
◇ Informed as to construction materials and purchasing procedures.

CAREER EMPLOYMENT HISTORY

1978 to
present

BUNTER FLASHMAN CONSTRUCTION
Operations Management

Construction analysis, site management and operations supervision
(multi/single family homes).

Vendor/client recruitment. Sales force development, with emphasis on
marketing.

Project management services: Provide supervision of all building and inspection phases.

Land acquisitions and site services including research and site-inspection
for prospective construction.

Modular unit settings. Provide in-house, sub-contracted crews and
equipment for completion.

Marketing and speculation units for pre-construction sales (single/multi
family).

EDUCATION

MOUNTAIN REALTY ACADEMY, Aurora, CO
Colorado Real Estate License 1983

Order Processing Manager

James Sharpe
9 Central Avenue
Nashville, TN 37222
(615) 555-1212

EXPERIENCE:

5/84 - Present   ORDER PROCESSING MANAGER
Marketing Masters, Nashville, TN

* Report to Director of Operations.
* Oversee all functions of the Network Mail Order Processing Department, including reservations, firm orders, cancellations, contract review and category exclusivity.
* Act as Liaison between Account Executives and Layout Department in the supervision of program development.
* Apprise Senior Management of weekly business activity, including firm and cancelled orders.
* Instituted new departmental procedures to more effectively meet business requirements.
* Directed Systems Manager in the development and implementation of a direct mail order processing computer system

2/83-5/84   TV MARKETING RESEARCH ANALYST
Rothen Public Relations, Nashville, TN

* Assisted Account Executives in planning client presentations.
* Calculated marketing variables such as product sales, market shares, percent changes; category and brand development indices; month's supply; advertising expenditures.
* Acted as Liaison between Client Service and Production Offices.
* Investigated unusual data or trends.
* Maintained electronic data base.

11/78-2/83   JEWELRY SALES REPRESENTATIVE
Southern Belle Accessories, Memphis, TN

* Assisted wholesale clients in the selection of their gold and silver product lines.
* Acted as Marketing Coordinator for several trade shows including the National Boutique Show (New York Colisseum, 1981).

EDUCATION: Manhattan College, Riverdale, New York
Bachelor of Science Degree (Business Administration) Cum Laude. 1978
Marketing Major - 4.0 GPA
Computer Information Systems Minor - 3.8 GPA

REFERENCES: Available upon request.

Paralegal

James Sharpe, 9 Central Avenue, Cleveland, OH 44115. (216) 555-1212

EXPERIENCE: **Robert Schoenberg P.C. Cleveland, OH**
Paralegal

Responsibility for various financial aspects of the partnership; organized the office work schedule. Answered the calendar calls in motion part, argued the motions and adjourned cases when necessary; conferenced cases in pre-trial procedure.

Drafted summons and complaints, subpoena duces tecum and judicial subpoena, answers to interrogatories and all notices of discovery.

Reviewed experts' reports and evaluated their relevance in the case.

Prepared clients for examinations before trial and city hearings.

1984 - Present

Appellate Division Municipal Court of Hong Kong
Judicial Assistant
Participated in civil and criminal trials; took depositions. Drafted the court decisions.
1966 - 1972

EDUCATION: **Brooklyn Law School**, Brooklyn, New York
 Graduated with diploma in Foreign Trained Lawyers Program
 February, 1984
Ohio State Bar Examination taken in July, 1987
Bernard Baruch College of the City University of New York
 Paralegal Studies
 Certified as a Paralegal in August, 1984
University of Hong Kong
 Faculty of Law
 Master of Arts - Specialty: Law. February, 1971

SKILLS   Fluent in Japanese and several Chinese dialects
Freelance writer for Asian newspapers published in the United States.
Translator from above languages into English and visa versa.

Payroll/Accounts Payable Supervisor

James Sharpe
9 Central Avenue
Campbell, CA 95008
(408) 555-1212

PROFESSIONAL BACKGROUND

1979 to
Present

WHOLEFOODS NC., Campbell, CA
Food Processing and Distributing

Payroll/Accounts Payable Supervisor (1984 to Present)
Supervised accounts payable personnel and reviewed their daily work . . .
Utilized IBM/3, Model 15 computer system for various accounting functions . . .
Managed, calculated, and maintained weekly payroll records for 400 employees
(800-900 at height of business) . . . Prepared weekly Federal, FICA, and State
withholding deposits . . . Prepared monthly health and welfare, and pension
reports . . . Delegated monthly bank reconciliations and reviewed work . . .
Prepared monthly account analysis (detailing and verifying the general ledger
balance sheet accounts).

Accounts Payable Clerk (1981 to 1984)
Checked vendor invoices for accuracy . . . Matched the invoice with the receiver
and purchase order . . . Prepared the accounts payable voucher and entered the
information into the CRT . . . Recorded cash receipts and disbursements and
prepared the monthly journal entry.

Accounts Receivable Clerk (1980 to 1981)
Processed and reviewed accounts receivable billing for one thousand customers
. . . Applied customer payments and charges . . . Reconciled accounts on a
monthly basis.

Cashier (1979 to 1980)
Reconciled and deposited cash from driver salespeople on a daily basis . . .
Calculated product sales per each driver and sales account.

EDUCATIONAL BACKGROUND

COMMERCE HIGH SCHOOL, Campbell, CA
Graduate of Business Program.

PERSONAL INFORMATION

Married with two children . . . Health is excellent . . . Height 5'5" . . . Weight 140
lbs.

REFERENCES

Furnished upon request.

James Sharpe
9 Central Avenue
Bridgeview, IL
(312) 555-1212

EXPERIENCE: Hughes Ovens & Hewitt, Bridgeview, IL

9/79 - Present

<u>Personnel Administrator</u>
<u>Support Staff Management</u>
Duties include:
- support staff recruiting
- supervision of secretarial assignments and group leaders
- coordination of work flow
- supervision of night secretarial staff
- coordination of freelance and temporary staff
- support staff orientation and training
- coordination of payroll process with accounting department
- analysis of personnel data for staffing and planning
- assistance with year-end evaluations and salary review

<u>Legal Recruiter</u>
Duties include:
- presentation of weekly status reports to Recruiting Committee
- coordination of interview schedules
- organization of orientation programs for incoming attorneys
- review and screening all incoming resumes
- processing all correspondence with law schools and individual applicants
- organization of social functions

<u>Benefits Administration</u>
Duties include:
- administration of health benefits including medical, life and short and long term disability
- administration of general insurance including personal and professional liability, and workmen's compensation

10/77 - 9/79

University of Chicago
<u>Coordinator of Loans</u>
- responsible for processing all accounts receivable for long-term student loans

EDUCATION:

University of Chicago
B.A., June 1981
Majors: Economics and Political Science
Minor: Computer Science

Bilingual (Spanish/English)

REFERENCES: Will be furnished upon request.

Personnel Assistant

Jane Swift
9 Central Avenue
Wheaton, IL 60187
(312) 555-1212

PROFESSIONAL OBJECTIVE

A challenging position and active involvement in a progressive organization offering the opportunity to fully utilize proven and developing people-oriented skills in the area of Human-Resources.

SUMMARY OF SUPPORTIVE QUALIFICATIONS

A results-oriented self-starter with highly developed administrative, problem-solving, and decision-making skills, including: Wage administration, personnel policies, staffing, benefit plans, performance appraisals and EEO.

WORK HISTORY

Personnel Assistant - JENKINS CAPACITORS, Wheaton, IL

March 1985 to Present: Assist the Vice President/Personnel in the administration of all personnel functions. Duties include recruiting, interviewing, hiring, writing and evaluating job descriptions. Administering the health care plans and other employee benefits, developing and administering the Affirmative Action Plan and the Performance Appraisal Program. Handle employee problems and interface with personnel from other companies.

Wage Administration Specialist - BELUSHI Inc. Wheaton, IL

December 1973 to 1985. Audited and processed weekly changes in wages and job status new hires and transfers for all nonexempt employees. Maintained job and rate history, wrote and evaluated job descriptions, conducted studies on wages and benefits and administered the annual wage and benefit survey conducted by the company. Interfaced with personnel from other departments and in the absence of the supervisor, was responsible for the functions of the department.

EDUCATION

1983   Wheaton State College, Wheaton, IL. Computer Principles Assertiveness Training. Effective Listening. Multi-Mate Word Processing. Affirmative Action/EEO Seminar. Personnel Diagnostics. Interviewing Workshop. Basic Personnel Administration. Your Employees and the Law.

PROFESSIONAL AFFILIATIONS

Personnel Management Association

Physical Therapist

James Sharpe
9 Central Avenue
Westerville, OH 43801
(614) 555-1212

OBJECTIVE

To acquire a clinical position in a Physical Therapy facility emphasizing Orthopaedics and Sports Medicine, while continuing to develop my interests in manual therapy.

EXPERIENCE

Cleveland General, 844-bed acute care facility, 6/87 to present. Staff therapist with responsibilities for managing outpatient department, supervising aides. Clinical instructor for graduate and baccalaureate students. Worked closely with a neurosurgeon in developing an exercise regime for post-op back fusion patients.

Middleburg Hospital, 325-bed acute care facility 3/83-6/87 Responsible for total in- and outpatient physical therapy care with participation in a Sports Medicine clinic, home care, and Cybex evaluations. In addition, handled burn and multiple-trauma patients.

EDUCATION

University of Ohio. Bachelor of Science in Physical Therapy, 1983

PROFESSIONAL ORGANIZATIONS

Member, American Physical Therapy Association
American Heart Association-Basic CPR certification

REFERENCES

Available upon request

Plastics Engineer

Jane Swift
9 Central Avenue
Beaumont, Texas 77705
(409) 555-1212

EXPERIENCE:

June 1983 to present - CONSUMER PACKAGING Inc., Beaumont, TX

Senior Research and Development Engineer (3/85 to present)

Responsible to three General Managers: (1) Plastic Development; (2) Technology Development; and (3) Business development for new and existing packaging. Development is centered around shelf stable food packaging. High degree of customer interaction: Responsible for customer technology acceptance.

Major achievements include: Direct involvement in promoting and implementing Nabisco's "Picnic Gourmet" package and Campbell Soup's "Cooks Kitchen" retortable crocks. Meet with potential customers to discuss concepts and make proposals. Prepare proposals, including tooling costs, design time frame, package costs, and equipment costs.

Research Engineer (5/84 to 3/85)

Held development responsibilities for dual injection molding program. Project leader concerning polymers selection, testing and tooling design. Responsible for taking concept into prototype and semi-production state.

Production Supervisor (6/83 to 5/84)

Directly responsible for plastic enclosure engineering development and production. Responsibilities included injection molding, polymer testing and selection. Product tooling engineering and design, ancillary engineering and purchasing, and financial project planning. In-depth research of mold monitoring systems, heaters, pressure transducers, temperature controllers and process controls for state-of-the-art injection molding operations.

March 1982 to June 1983 - BELL INDUSTRIES - MOULDING DIVISION, San Francisco, CA

Process Engineer

Responsible to Production Manager for technical supervision of modern, state-of-the-art molding department, comprising a 200 employee manufacturing facility. Responsibilities included scheduling and instruction of personnel, preparing daily production reports, maintaining inventory, providing technical expertise, troubleshooting, and ordering and assisting in design of auxiliary equipment.

EDUCATION:
1981 - B.S. Industrial Plastics; Illinois State University
Minor: Business Administration

Process Control Engineer

James Sharpe
9 Central Avenue
Horsham, PA 19044
(215) 555-1212

OBJECTIVE:

Seeking a position in computer engineering. While interested in software development, microprocessor applications, and networking, I am flexible on the specific nature of work.

**SOFTWARE/
HARDWARE**

UNIX, StarLAN Applications, C Language, MS-DOS 3.1, Square D Programmable Controller (PLC) with Ladder Logic Programming, Square D SY/NET Data Network, Texas Instruments PLC Boolean Logic Programming, Basic, AutoCAD, Nitto Seiko Robots using PTP Programming Formats.

**WORK
EXPERIENCE:**

1985 to Present: Global-Tel, Philadelphia, PA

Process Control Engineer involved with the implementation of two automatic assembly systems for production of computer keyboards. Responsibilities include:

- Programming of the 26 S.C.A.R.A. robots on assembly lines. Developing process control programs to implement total control of production, and selecting all electrical apparatus associated with the operations of the assembly lines.

- Design of several other process controls systems for additonal automatic assembly units, and extensive development work on an automatic test station for keyboard switches.

1984 to 1985: University of Pennsylvania, EE Dept.

Research Student Designed a computer-based clinical audiometer to allow ear specialists flexibility with decibel and frequency ranges in patient testing.

This provided the capability to transform frequency signals with other waveforms to perform developmental tests on hearing response. Design was performed using an Intel 8088 microprocessor, with digital-to-analog technology.

EDUCATION:

University of Pennsylvania
B.S. Electrical Engineering   G.P.A. 3.86 of 4.0
Valedictorian

Product Development Engineer

Jane Swift
9 Central Avenue
KANSAS CITY, MO 64108
(816) 555-1212

OBJECTIVE: A challenging opportunity as Senior Staff Engineer or Project Leader in-
                  volved with new product development.

SOFTWARE: C, Pascal, FORTRAN, COBOL, LISP, Assemblers; UNIX System 5.2, 5.3;
                  UNIX Kernal and UNIX Tools.

EXPERIENCE:

5/83 - Present. WORKHORSE/MONEYMAKER SOFTWARE. Staff Engineer

Responsibilities have entailed design through implementation of front end modules for new product development. Specifically developed

* A command interpreter, menu system, help facility, utilities, tools and
  library routines.

* A modified A terminal driver within the operating system. Work uses C
  language on the Motorola 68000 under UNIX.

* As a member of the advanced Development Group, researched and
  selected alternate peripheral devices including larger disks, a laser
  printer, and scanners.

* Developed a data collection system using C under UNIX 5.2. Functioned
  as technical advisor, provided training and support to a group of eight
  software engineers.

1980 - 1982. UNIVERSITY OF VIRGINIA. Graduate Research Assistant

* Adapted the UNIX operating system to Prime equipment. Set up a
  restricted UNIX environment for a programming course. Taught COBOL
  and worked as a Grader/Consultant for Pascal.

EDUCATION: University of Virginia.
                  M.S.Computer Science '82.
                  B.A., Cum Laude '78.

Project Leader

James Sharpe
9 Central Avenue
Miami, FL 33161
(305) 555-1212

OBJECTIVE: To locate a challenge for a superior Senior Programmer/Analyst or Project Leader utilizing hands-on expertise in IDMS applications development.

SUMMARY: Six years' progressive experience in programming financial and insurance applications using IDMS, COBOL, and structured programming and design techniques in both batch and on-line environments.

HARDWARE: IBM 3083, 43x, 370.

SOFTWARE: COBOL; CICS, TSO/SPF, IDMS, ADS-on line (ADSO), On-Line Mapping (OLM), CULPRIT, ACF, OS/VS2, MVS, IMS.

EXPERIENCE: *AIR FLORIDA*

1981 - Present *Programmer/Analyst* - Participated in the development of two major on-line projects utilizing IDMS, ADSO, and OLM. These projects included time/cost estimates, system design, screen design, report layouts, functional and technical analysis and specifications, programming, testing, implementation and system documentation.

Responsibilities included purchasing, tailoring, interfacing and implementing an IDMS General Ledger software package. Interfaced with user community and support personnel, and provided user training on a functional level. Extensive knowledge and experience with IDMS, ADSO, OLM, ACF, CULPRIT, and SPF.

1979 - 1981 *STATE FARM INSURANCE*

Programmer/Analyst - Responsibilities included maintaining, enhancing and supporting group insurance applications. Specifically, handled analysis, programming and testing using structured methodologies and data base systems. Worked closely with users to define and support their needs. Project supervision and training responsibilities for three junior programmers.

EDUCATION: B.S. (Computer Communications) 1979, City University of New York

REFERENCES: Available upon request.

Jane Swift
9 Central Avenue
Bridgeview, IL 60455
(312) 555-1212

HARDWARE:	DEC VAX 11/780, System 10, PDP-11/45, PDP-8, Prime 850, 750, 550; IBM 360
SOFTWARE:	VMS (RMS), TOPS-10, TSX-11M, DOS, PRIMOS, Prime Information, TAPR; Knowledge of Datatrieve
LANGUAGES:	COBOL, Info/BASIC, MACRO-11, DCL, GEOMAP, RPG, FORTRAN, Easycoder
EXPERIENCE:	BankSafe Software Inc., Chicago, IL.

7/83 - Present   Senior Programmer/Analyst - Involved in the design and development of Financial Software targeted for the banking industry. Write applications for: Product creation, fee and index processing. Also involved with tape processing for third-party sources: Credit Agencies; IRS, and Social Security. Language: COBOL Hardware: DEC VAX 11/780.

Illinois Education Assistance Corporation, Chicago, IL.

1982 - 1983   Programmer/Analyst - Participated in the design of reports and statistical analyses and in format conversion of the GSLP (Guaranteed Student Loan Program) System. Responsible for some documentation. Language: COBOL Hardware: Prime 750, 550.

CITY OF CHICAGO, MIS DEPARTMENT.

1977 - 1980   Programmer II - Promoted to this position after one year as Programmer I. Project leader for Payroll System. Lead Programmer in planning stages of conversion for all systems from DEC-10 to Univac.

Programmer I - Participated in design and programming for Task Accounting and Reporting applications. Programmed for Computer Assisted Appraisal and Elections application. Wrote user guide for data entry. Language: COBOL Hardware: DEC System 10

EDUCATION: B.S. Computer Engineering, University of Lowell, Lowell, MA.

Public Relations/Media Spokesperson

JANE SWIFT
9 Central Avenue
Phoenix, AZ 85016
(602) 555-1212

OBJECTIVE:

A position in Public Relations where I can utilize my skills as a media spokesperson and my ability to execute a variety of projects simultaneously.

EXPERIENCE:

Public Relations Associate/Media
ADRIENNE ARPEL. Phoenix, AZ. 1986 to Present

* Media spokesperson for 12 western states: Interviewed and trained personnel for TV, radio and print
* Established contacts with producers and editors
* Wrote press releases
* Developed media and promotional packages
* Booked interviews with press

District Sales Manager
ADRIENNE ARPEL. Phoenix, AZ. 1983 - 1986

* Supervised 169 representatives with a $500,000 sales volume.

Account Executive/Radio Reporter
KTUV RADIO. Phoenix, AZ. 1980 - 1983

* Designed and sold advertising for KTUV Radio
* Developed a $9,000 account list in the Phoenix metro market
* Sports and news announcer (included in-studio as well as location)
* Traffic reporter

Assistant Editor
Daily Arqus Observer, Ontario, OR. Summers 1978/1979

* Feature writer, reporter, photographer, layouts and design

EDUCATION:

B.S. Speech Communications, University of Arizona, 1980.

AWARDS:

1988 Arizona Business and Professional Women's "Young Careerist" Annual Award

OTHER FACTS:

Experience as a Public Relations Seminar Leader

References/Portfolio/Video and Cassette Tapes available upon request

Publishing/Marketing Professional

Jane Swift
9 Central Avenue
Seacliff, NY 11579
(516) 555-1212

PROFESSIONAL EXPERIENCE:

A New York Publisher of trade and scholarly books
DIRECTOR OF ADVERTISING AND PROMOTION (March 1986-Present)

Key responsibilities include: managing advertising/promotion department with staff of four; overseeing and actively engaging in all aspects of promotion, advertising, and publicity. I have established and am maintaining a 22-person national sales force and make seasonal visits to the nation's two largest bookstore chains.

Active in negotiating special sales, acquiring new titles, and as liaison with domestic and foreign rights agents. In 1985 I traveled to England, visited several publishers, bought and sold rights.

Frequently arrange author appearances on television and radio talk shows. As a company spokesperson, I have been interviewed numerous times by newspapers, magazines, syndicates, and radio stations.

ADVERTISING AND PROMOTION MANAGER (1984-1986)

Advertising and Direct Mail: Created, designed, and wrote copy for brochures, flyers, and display ads; created direct mail campaigns; represented company at publisher's book exhibits.

Publicity: Wrote news releases, selected media, made follow-up calls, arranged author media appearances.

ASSISTANT EDITOR (1982-1984)

Responsibilities included reading authors' manuscripts, copy editing, proofreading; writing jacket copy, coordinating and writing copy for catalog. Some editing and proofreading was done on a free-lance basis.

Compton Burnett. (New York, NY) **ADVERTISING COPYWRITER (1978-1982)**

Responsible for designing and writing copy for bimonthly catalog and supplementary flyers. Created ads and brochures; wrote sales letters, and edited and rewrote direct mail pieces.

EDUCATION:

State University of New York at Buffalo
Degree: B.A. in English, 1978
Minor: Social Sciences

SKILLS:

Typing, word processing, working knowledge of typography, research proficiency.

REFERENCES:

Will be provided on request.

Quality Control Manager

James Sharpe
9 Central Avenue
Kenner, LA 70062
(504) 555-1212

Career Objective:
Quality Control Manager with a food industry leader

Employment Experience.

Firebird Kitchens/Athens, Kenner, LA

Quality Control Director: Supervise Quality Control Department. Responsible for Research & Development and interaction with USDA program. Products include chicken and dumplings, noodles with chicken, canned deboned chicken, and barbecued chicken. July 1985 to Present.

Green Valley Canning Company, Jackson, FL

Quality Control Supervisor: Manage Quality Control program and assist the Plant Manager in planning and monitoring the production of dry bean products (canned & packaged), fruit juice, tortilla chips and canned whole kernel corn. Responsible for product development and improvement of existing products. February 1983 to July 1985

Stauffers, Inc. Cleveland, OH 1971-1982

Quality Control Technologist: Supervised the Quality Control at Possum Trot plant. Assigned to two seasonal plants in Kentucky during the summer. 1978 to 1982

Laboratory Assistant: Performed laboratory procedures and supervised the Quality Control Technicians. 1976-1978

Assembler and Machine Inspector. 1974 to August 1976

Education & Vocational Skills:

University of Louisiana. Better Process Control School

Kenner Technical Institute. Major: Laboratory Technician and Management-Food Science

Food Chemistry, Communications, Nutrition, Quality control, Food Microbiology, Technical Math, Supervision, First Aid, Food Preservation, Laboratory Procedures.

Willing to relocate. References available.

Real Estate Professional

James Sharpe
9 Central Avenue
Anaheim, CA 92803
(714) 555-1212

EDUCATION:

Law:
: Cornell LAW SCHOOL,
Juris Doctor. Conferred May 1987
Cum Laude, Grade Point Average: 3.5
Client Counseling Competition - Quarter-finalist
Course Emphasis: Land Use/Environmental Law

Undergraduate:
: CORNELL UNIVERSITY
B.A. 1985
Concentrations: Environmental/Urban Policy

EMPLOYMENT:

May 1987
to
Present
: *Gerould, Zanke and Chivers. Anaheim, CA*

Associate. Commercial Real Estate and Lending. Draft and negotiate loan documents. Advise lenders on various hazardous waste and land use issues. Review opinions of borrower's counsel relating to perfection of security interests, zoning and environmental and land use, corporate authority, and enforceability and secured transactions issues. Prepare and negotiate commercial purchase and sale agreements.

Spring 1987
: *ATTORNEY GENERAL OF NEW YORK, Albany, NY*

Legal intern with Public Protection Bureau. Significant participation in litigation and research.

Fall 1986
: *Kettering,Channel & Bly, Carle Place, NY*

Legal intern. Assisted attorneys. Research in environmental law. Significant contact with public agencies.

Summer 1986
: *CORNELL LAW JOURNAL*

Researched and developed topics for publication.

JANE SWIFT
9 Central Avenue
Charlotte, NC 28210
(704) 555-1212

OBJECTIVE

A challenging sales/sales management opportunity, utilizing my ability to stimulate and motivate a productive sales force. An opportunity in which I can significantly contribute to an employer through increase in sales volume and profit.

EXPERIENCE

A Merrill Lynch Affiliate, Charlotte, NC
Largest, oldest real estate sales office, producing highest sales volume for the Charlotte area.

Manager, 1984 - present
Salesperson, 1976 - 1984
Direct and coordinate all activities of 8-person sales office. Train in effective telephone canvassing techniques, and methods to accurately evaluate homes. Develop ways to expedite and effect the closing of the sales.

Form sales teams within office, establish sales quotas for inter-office contests, motivate staff individually and in groups. Annual turnover reduced from 60% to 18%, while individual production increased 33%.

Consistently secure all saleable exclusive and multiple listings, follow up to establish company credibility and the rapport essential to retaining clients in a competitive marketplace. Exclusives increased 45% under my management.

Negotiate final sale price, date of possession, secure most appropriate lending institution for buyers. Deal personally with real estate attorneys, devising contracts for consummation of sale.

Evaluate homes as prospects for company purchase for speculative purposes. Personally responsible for decisions to buy, rendering of dollar offer, initiating activity for resale.

Develop copy and photographs of homes for major advertising publications.

TRAINING

Dale Carnegie Institute, 1977: Seminar series for sales, closing and negotiating. Various additional courses and seminars to instill, polish and perfect skills in salesmanship.

Jane Swift
9 Central Avenue
Dayton, OH 45426
(513) 555-1212

EXPERIENCE
Dayton Thread Company, Inc.
19 McKeon Road, Worcester, MA.
7/85 - present   Receptionist/Clerk
2/82 - 6/85   Assistant Sales Coordinator/Secretary

Job
Summary
All-inclusive typing for six people - President, Vice Presidents, Treasurer, Sales Coordinator and Credit Manager

Customer Service - writing orders, checking orders, advising customers, etc.

Order Process - writing orders, numbering products, customer coding, pricing, checking computer edit, adding poundage, etc.

TWX Operator, Opening Accounts

Brattle Street Market
1 Brattle Street, Worcester, MA.
Part Time Employment
Service Clerk - Cashier, Waitress & other hospitality duties. 3/77 - 2/82

Skills
Type 65 wpm

Upon completion of Advanced College Shorthand, could take shorthand at the rate of 110 wpm.

REFERENCES:
Gladly furnished upon request

Jane Swift
9 Central Avenue
Glenhead, NY 11579
(516) 555-1212

EMPLOYMENT
OBJECTIVE: Supervisor of filing and records management

EMPLOYMENT:
Getchell & Getchell, New York, NY

Assistant Supervisor - Maintaining a large number of client documents, utilizing an alphabetized system; assigning daily workload to clerks; light typing; responsible for processing audit letters to assist partners in regulating billing procedures; some experience in conducting cost analysis for supplies. July 1984 to Present

Hardy, Hardy, and Hardy, New York, NY

Assistant Supervisor - Duties consisted of filing and recording documents for United States Trust Company of New York and all other clients in such legal areas as corporate, trusts and estates, litigation and general matters utilizing an alpha-numeric system; responsible for setting up and coordinating new matters; culling out non-active files for delivery to storage; experience in the field of researching and use of law library in conjunction with attorney request; knowledgeable in the performance of light typing tasks. February 1981 to June 1984

EDUCATION:
Adelphi University, Spring Semester, 1983
Generalist course of study of the Lawyer's Assistant program.

Notary Public - New York County

Member of ARMA (Association of Record Managers and Administrators)

REFERENCES: Furnished upon request.

Research Scientist

Jane Swift, 9 Central Avenue, Ft. Lauderdale, FL 33309. (305 555-1212)

EXPERIENCE:

1984 to present - OWN BRAND FOODS, FL. Research Scientist
Current responsibilities include: developing new products for the Fresh
Meats division and supervising operational implementation. Specific duties
include:

> *Providing input for generation of product concept; bench-top
> formulation; pilot plant testing; sensory evaluation;
> coordination of package development; development of quality
> control programs.
>
> *Supervision of quality control personnel and three lab
> technicians in the corporate research laboratory. Production
> scale-ups in plants; and trouble-shooting operational problems.
>
> *Extensive experience in formulating foods specifically for
> microwave cooking.

ACCOMPLISHMENTS:

> *Developed a square bacon product sold to Wendy's Restaurants.
>
> *Developed 5 pre-cooked entrees sold to Stouffers.
>
> *Developed several pre-packaged retail cuts, currently in test
> market.

1977 to 1982 - University of Nebraska. Research Assistant

Meat Science Research duties included planning, implementing and analyzing
data for a variety of meat research products. Teaching assistant for
introductory and advanced meats classes. Assisted with various consumer
oriented programs.

EDUCATION:

> 1982 - University of Nebraska - Lincoln, PhD
> 1979 - University of Nebraska - Lincoln, MS
> 1977 - Auburn University, BS-Food Science

PROFESSIONAL MEMBERSHIPS:

> American Meat Science Association
> Institute of Food Technologists

Publication list and references available upon request.

Jane Smith
9 Central Avenue
Ft. Lauderdale, FL 33309
(305) 555-1212

Seeking a retail management position that allows for career growth.

WORK EXPERIENCE

**6/84-
Present**

Sales Manager, Penney's: Ft. Lauderdale
Manage eleven dress departments and five coat departments. Supervise and motivate thirteen associates. Maintain excellent customer service. Ensure proper merchandise presentation on selling floor.

Review and react to merchandise information reports, establishing trends and best-selling items. Communicate with central merchants, as well as store managers and selling personnel. Control individual department inventory. **Management evaluation, "Excellent."**

**2/81-
6/84**

Assistant Buyer Sportswear Macy's. Ft. Lauderdale
Facilitate prompt flow of departmental merchandise. Ensure accuracy of paperwork and inventory control. Maintain efficient vendor and branch store communication. Review stock levels and merchandise assortment. Track departmental trends. **Supervisor evaluation: "Superior performance."**

**5/77-
2/81**

Secretary. Bergdorf Goodman, Ft. Lauderdale
Secretary to store executives, orientation of new employees. Exposed to operational management. Work closely with assistant store managers. Familiar with compensation and insurance plans, payroll procedures, employee reviews, and customer service, including customer complaints and billing. **Performance evaluation: "Outstanding."**

**12/73-
5/77**

Sales, Maxim's. Ft. Lauderdale
Worked closely with Fashion. Prepare layout and merchandise display. **Performance evaluation: "Excellent."**

Sales Support/Administration Specialist

Jane Swift
9 Central Avenue
Dallas, TX 75247
(214) 555-1212

OBJECTIVE: Management responsibility with an organization where demonstrated skills in Marketing, Administration and Sales can be translated into improved growth and profitability.

BACKGROUND SUMMARY Twelve years' business experience with increasing responsibility in Marketing, Finance, Personnel, Data Processing, Sales Administration functions. A thorough knowledge of all office procedures, Board of Directors meeting administration, sales/revenue/financial analysis, brochure/catalog preparation, trade show/seminar coordination.

EXPERIENCE:

DEVON PHARMACEUTICALS INC. Dallas, TX. (12/82-Present)
Sales Support Administrator.

Act on behalf of the Director in his absence and direct all matters for proper resolution. "Special projects" and committee assignments comprise the major portion of this position, including

> Coordination of company relocation to a new facility, with five concurrent annual company functions.

> Coordinate the conversion to a new archival system

> Control activities with executive search firms and interview candidates while under re-organization.

> Develop and revise corporate policies and procedures; and participate in a variety of special acquisition proposals for the Board of Directors.

> Prepare, administer and assist in the analysis of the Annual Employee Salary Review Program.

THE CUBBISON COMPANY. Dallas, TX (6/79 - 4/82)
Market Development Analyst

Investigate and recommend new programs and channels of distribution to increase revenue. Recommend new products for re-sale.

Administrative Assistant to General Manager

Coordinate revenue vs. plan reports as well as Marketing staff programs for division's branch offices. Input intelligence on competitive activity. Formalized divisional level personnel policies and procedures.

EDUCATION: BS/BA, Marketing, 1978. Smith College (Northampton, MA)

Salesperson

Jane Swift
9 Central Avenue
Mount Vernon, NY 10550
(914) 555-1212

OBJECTIVE

To obtain a challenging position in Marketing or Sales, providing an opportunity to apply skills and interest in Sales, Promotions, Customer Service and related ideas.

QUALIFICATIONS

Retail Sales and Customer Service, in consumer products and services; dealt on an individual basis to help customers meet their needs. Ultimately responsible for customer satisfaction. Served also in the hospitality business.

As *Marketing Consultant* to retail businesses, have conceived, developed, produced and executed advertising campaigns and promotional activities. Created advertising themes, wrote copy, prepared designs and graphics, made media decisions, subcontracted art and production, and placed advertising. Successfully developed programs within budgets and deadlines.

Developed *Promotions* and promotional campaigns, including a contest to name a new business, promoting a recreational league, publicizing the activities of a professional organization, including publicity support for a continuing lecture program.

Other Responsibilities: organize, plan and carry out programs (including recruitment, scheduling and financing); communicate with and teach patients health care practices; serve in several offices of a professional organization, with responsibility for organizing and carrying out activities; perform volunteer work, teaching and training in schools and youth groups.

WORK HISTORY
Marketing Consultant - 1985 to present

Spanky's Casuals, White plains, NY
Retail Sales, Customer Service, 1980 to 1984

Crazy Eddie Electronics, NY, NY
Retail Sales, Customer Service 1972 to 1979

EDUCATION

New York Institute of Technology
A.S., , with additional courses in Business Law, and Computer Science.

Senior Executive Secretary

Jane Swift
9 Central Avenue
Austin, TX 78745
(512) 555-1212

<u>SUMMARY:</u>

Depth of experience: Business management, business systems analysis, and communications. Areas of expertise include typing, shorthand, accounting, and dealing with confidential material generated by Executive Officers.

<u>KEY QUALIFICATIONS:</u>

Self-motivated - experience in instituting and conducting all phases of office procedures, organizing and coordinating projects for maximum efficiency.

Progressive development of excellent interpersonal and communication skills.

Demonstrated record of high performance standards, including attention to schedules, deadlines, budgets and quality of work.

Ability to work independently and institute creative improvements which allow better management work flow.

<u>CAREER HISTORY:</u>

<u>Minsky Management, Austin, TX</u> - 1983 - Present. A Property Management Co.

Senior Executive Secretary. Duties include all daily administrative and secretarial work, accounts receivable, accounts payable, general ledgers, payroll, including monthly deposits and quarterly returns as well as quarterly tax estimates. Responsible for maintaining records and reconciling monthly statements for 36 investment accounts, 20 checking accounts, and 24 savings accounts.

Manage all real estate for six shopping centers, including leases, rents, common area maintenance charges and mortgage payments which include verification of interest and principal amounts. Interact and correspond with tenants.

Co-ordinate travel arrangements.

Responsible for special projects as assigned.

<u>Mr. Gatti's Inc. Austin, TX</u>. 1970 - 1983. Pizza Franchisor

Office Manager, Assistant Treasurer, Duties included all daily administrative and secretarial work, accounts receivable, accounts payable, accounting through trial balance and payroll including monthly deposits and quarterly returns. Handled all banking, including loans and trade acceptances. Interacted and corresponded with customers and vendors.

<u>EDUCATION</u>

Auburn High School - Honor Graduate
IBM Award - Outstanding Business Student
NASD License

Senior Payroll Clerk

Jane Swift
9 Central Avenue
Chicago, Il 60601
(312) 555-1212

EXPERIENCE
1980 to
Present

Washington Construction. Chicago.
Senior Payroll Clerk

Duties and Responsibilities: Processing of hourly employees' wages. Closing and balancing weekly, monthly and year-end work. Health and Dental Insurance, processing various payroll reports, organizing weekly, monthly and yearly records, balancing petty cash, issuing traveler's checks, handling cash receipts and cash disbursements.

Accounts Payable Clerk

Duties and Responsibilities: Recording receivings, answering questions for customers, posting material paid, filing, typing, processing mail, processing invoices to be paid, balancing purchases at month end, and assisting auditors at year end.

BUSINESS SKILLS

Competent with IBM Sys 11 and compatibles, VisiCalc and Lotus 123. Typing speed: 60 W.P.M, (IBM, Adler, Olympia). Electronic calculators, adding machines, teletype, and check writer.

EDUCATION
1982
to Present

Chicago City College
Business Courses: Data Processing, Macroeconomics, Cost Accounting, Payroll, Intermediate Accounting, Accounting Principles I and II, Typewriting, Business Communications, Data Processing, Business Organization (Income Tax, Economics and Business Law)

REFERENCES

Will be furnished upon request.
Attended Seminar on Accounts Receivable, Credit and Collections once every two months for the past four years. I have contacted customers by telephone, telex, and/or wrote for collection of past due invoices. Also, contacted salespeople concerning problems with contracts and machinery parts.

Senior Systems Programmer

Jane Swift
9 Central Avenue
Salt Lake City, UT 84106
(801) 555-1212

SUMMARY:

With eight plus years of data processing experience comprising both operations and systems programming background, Jane Swift is a thoroughly knowledgeable Systems Programmer.

**HARDWARE/
SOFTWARE:**

308X, 303X, 370, System 34, 8100, 3725, P.C., OS/MVS, ASSEMBLER, CICS, RJE, JES II, SNA, ACF, VTAM, NCP, NPM, NPDA, MSNF, VSAM, NCCF, DISOSS, SNI, CNM, EREP, GTF, TSO/ISPF, SMP

EXPERIENCE:

Current Employer. A Technology Conglomerate.   *10/84 to Present*
Systems Programmer

Responsibilities include the installation and maintenance of networking software products (NCP, Version 3 NPDA, NPM, NCCF, etc.), supporting SNI, managing VSAM for CNM products, etc.

INCO Corporation   *7/81 to 10/84*

Systems Programmer   *11/83 to 10/84*

Installed and maintained NCCF, NPDA, DISOSS and EREP. Responsible for NCP generations and VTAM modifications. Worked with Support Center on assorted problems and disk problem determination using GTG and NCP dumps.

Operations Analyst   *9/83 to 11/83*

Responsible for training computer operators in networking; wrote network operations procedure manual with trouble-shooting flowcharts.

Network Operator   *7/81 to 9/83*

Gained hands-on experience with ACF/VTAM, NCP environment. Installed IBM terminals, modems and 3274 control units. Used modem tests and datascope to work with AT&T on communication problems.

EDUCATION: *C.W. Post College*
B.S. - Data Processing. 1984.

Software Engineer

Jane Swift, 9 Central Avenue, Yonkers, NY 10701. (914) 555-1212

OBJECTIVE: Challenging opportunity as Software Engineer utilizing expertise in C/UNIX programming.

HARDWARE: M68000 Series; DEC VAX 11/750, PDP 11/34; IBM PC.

SOFTWARE: C, Intel 8086 Assembler; UNIX 5.3, 5.2, 4.2,
VMS, MS/DOS. Pascal, LISP, Fortran
BASIC, Macro-II.

EXPERIENCE: **A Computer Peripheral Co.** 11/86 - Present

Engineer - Responsibilities include design, development and installation of a software product that polls virtually any type of remote computer on a scheduled basis. Function as primary interface with field personnel for support of this product.

Involved with porting UNIX utilities to the proprietary system and supporting these utilities. Developed a user interface embracing: Design and coding with C on M68000 under UNIX. Utilized the Courses Library to develop a windowing environment. All code has been designed and ported to the IBM PC-AT under MS/DOS.

Vector VISION SYSTEMS, INC. 1/85 - 11/86

Software Engineer - Developed an I/O interface between Intel 8086 software and 8031 firmware and developed numerous system test utilities for use on a PC Board Inspection System. Also provided overall maintenance of a M68000 super-micro running under UNIX.

NEW YORK UNIVERSITY. 6/82 - 1/85

Systems Programmer - Responsible for various projects related to system software development including debugging and implementing a file transfer package using C on DEC VAX 11/750. Also handled computer operations for two DEC PDP 11/34's and a DEC VAX 11/750 running under UNIX.

EDUCATION: B.A. degree in Computer Science. New York University. 1984

Staff Accountant/Real Estate

James Sharpe, 9 Central Avenue, Brooklyn, NY 11432. (212) 555-1212

OBJECTIVE: To obtain a responsible position in a company, where my experience, accomplishments, and proficiency will allow me the opportunity for growth.

STRENGTHS: Motivated, with highly concentrated learning curve. Astute technician, and personable. Stamina and know-how to undertake the most challenging situations.

EXPERIENCE:

1987 - present
CUSHMAN & WAKEFIELD, INC., New York City, NY
Staff Accountant
Accounting, financial, and planning responsibilities for 25 office buildings consisting of 25 to 100 tenants each.
Developed and implemented cash management procedures governing receipt, custody, and disbursements of funds.
Reviewed and verified rental condition reports to insure timely billing.
Acted as liaison with property manager, building manager and owner's representative. Prepared budget forecast for all properties.

1982-1987
PEN PLAZA, INC., New York City, NY
Collections Administrator
Monitored accounts receivable/accounts payable, recommended credit policies, collections, internal control implementation and administration. Planned and entered all credit/collection data into computer system. Conducted weekly staff meetings with account executives.
Identified and collected all delinquent accounts; established and proved timely payment plans.

1975-1982
THE IMPORT & EXPORT CO., New York City, NY
Accounting Clerk
Responsible for accounts receivable/accounts payable, general ledger, and processed payroll for 800 employees. Compiled and performed various bookkeeping functions for two subsidiary companies. Calculated and reported all state and federal taxes. Oversaw petty cash.

EDUCATION: Rutgers University, Newark, NJ
B.A. in Business Administration, 1974

REFERENCES: Available upon request

James Sharpe
9 Central Avenue
Oldsmar, FL 33557
(813) 555-1212

WORK EXPERIENCE

Manager. A National Kitchen Utensil Retailer. 1986-present. Manage daily operations of a 2-million annual business. Staff of 12 people. Responsible for increasing sales and profitability and decreasing expenses.

Increased gross margin by 25% and net contribution by 105% on a 3% sales increase.

Senior Assistant Buyer, Stern's. 1982 to 1986.
Control open to buy purchase journal, profitability reports, weekly three month estimate of sales, stocks, and markdown dollars. Plan and negotiate sales promotions, advertising, and special purchases.

Coordinate training and teamwork with managers and merchants in the 22 stores.

Increased department sales 18% more than the Division's increase.

Assistant Buyer. Assisted selection and distribution of merchandise. Managed all buying office functions while learning to plan sales, control stocks and markdown dollars. Create weekly, monthly, and seasonal financial plans.

Developed all systems to support the growth of the branch from a $1-million volume to a $4 million annual volume.

Buyer/Manager. Gulf Gifts FL 1979 to 1982.
Buy merchandise for two different gift stores. Direct daily store operations and sales. Direct merchandise presentation, inventory control, and customer service. Schedule and supervise a 7-person staff.

Increased sales volume 22% more than corporate projection.

Manager. Willis & Geiger, New York, NY 1976 to 1979.
Direct daily store operations. Analyze trends in fashion, merchandise, and consumer needs. Planned effective marketing strategy, displays, advertising, and an employee sales program.

Increased annual net sales volume by 33%.

EDUCATION

Fashion Institute of Technology, New York, NY. B.A. Merchandising, 1975

Systems Programmer

James Sharpe, 9 Central Avenue, Waterbury, VT 05676. (802) 555-1212

COMPUTER SYSTEMS	Apple Plus II Decsystem 20/60, IBM 370/158, MVS IBM 3081, MVS, TSO	NCR PC-4, PC-8, PDP 11-70, UNIX Compaq
COMPUTER LANGUAGES	Apple Assembler TI-990 Assembler NCR PC-8 Assembler IBM-370 Assembler APL BASIC	C COBOL Database: TOTAL, DBMS-20 FORTRAN NATURAL PASCAL

EXPERIENCE

SOFTWARE ENGINEER, Major Computer Co. 1986 to present

Designed and developed printer Basic Input/Output Service routines for 7052 (PC-8 based, IBM AT compatible) intelligent retail terminal. Used in-circuit emulator to debug software and software interface to hardware. *Key challenges* include re-entrancy, interrupt service routines, and power recovery.

Contributed to design of software interface to new multifunction printer. Met tight schedules for important product. Currently developing a printer driver in C for an 80188-based dumb retail terminal. Key challenge is providing application compatibility given new hardware. Project received quality awards.

SOFTWARE ENGINEER, Compaq, Houston, TX. 1985 - 1986.

Designed tests for single-user record operations and user interface for file manager on Compaq Personal Computer. Responsibility for directory and system generation utilities. Received Compaq employee appreciation award.

PROGRAMMER, Computer Consultants, Houston, TX. 1982 - 1985.

35 assignments, consisting of program changes, IBM JCL changes and creation, new program creation in NATURAL, IBM-370 assembler, and UNIX shell.

EDUCATION

B.S. COMPUTER SCIENCE, U.C./Berkeley. 1982

Systems Team Leader

James Sharpe
9 Central Avenue
Saginaw, MI 48090
(313) 555-1212

SUMMARY:
MIS specialist, experienced in both systems and applications areas. Major experience, strengths and skills are: Technical Supervision, Mapper, Telcon/CMS, OS 1100

EXPERIENCE:
1986-Present. Transmission Systems Inc. Troy, MI. Team Leader
Responsible for all aspects of the MIS group. Provided computer services for the company business applications.
* Total processing output increased 500% with very little increase in equipment cost.
* Produced a plan to purchase disk drives that would pay for themselves in less than 5 years by reducing maintenance costs.
* Designed and implemented an online stock system.

1983-1986. WarrenPower and Light Co., Troy, MI. Senior Systems Programmer
Responsible for all aspects of the software communications group. Provided communication services to over 1500 screens.
* Responsible for installation of communications when the company moved to multiple computer sites. This involved five high-speed UDLC lines.
* Responsible for the installation of three new DCP/40 front-end processors and one line switch module.
* Upgraded the network software to handle 300% increase in the number of terminals

1981-1983. Power Consulting Ltd. Detroit, MI. Senior Systems Analyst
Responsible for applications, systems design and implementations.
* Reduced cost of a major distribution system from over $200,000 to $25,000.
* Held Mapper run design classes.
* Designed, wrote and implemented cash flow analysis system for a multibillion-dollar company
* Responsible for several Mapper installations.
  Involved in several hardware and software conversions.

EDUCATION: B.S. in Business, City University of New York. 1980

Technical Services Manager

James Sharpe
9 Central Avenue
BEAVERTON, OR 97005
(503) 555-1212

SUMMARY:

Over 14 years of experience in Data Processing including Operations Management, Systems Programming, and Systems Programming Management. Technical experience includes three years of both NCP/VTAM and CICS systems programming as well as one year plus of MVS background.

**HARDWARE/
SOFTWARE:**

IBM 4341, 4381, Q14, 3380, 3375, 3705, VM/XA SF, MVS/XA, DOS/VSE, VM/SP, CICS, DL/1, IMS, VTAM, NCP, MSHP, SMP-E, TSO/ISPF PDF, MSA AP, MSA PAYROLL, EASYTRIEVE, ASSEMBLER, FAVER, UCCI

EXPERIENCE:

TECTRONIX. Manager, Technical Services. 11/86 to Present.

Plan and participate in the development and implementation of operating systems, data base systems and related software packages.

Guide, monitor and review the work of systems programming and data base administration.

Support of MVS/XA, VM/XA SF, utilizing SMP-E and related software maintenance utilities.

Responsible for the telecommunications environment supporting 350 terminal devices utilizing VTAM/NCP.

CHEMICAL BANK. Systems Programmer. 6/83 to 11/86.

Planned and executed the interstate move of the Corporate Data Center. Installation and testing of all new hardware and telecommunication lines in the new data center, as well as coordinating the movement of data between the two centers.

CICS and VTAM support.

Applications group support in the consolidation of four corporations, data processing operations onto a single set of business applications.

Project leader of MVS conversion project. Responsible for the planning and installation of MVS, CICS, IMS, and NCP utilizing CBIPO. Also for the planning and implementation of MVS and VM/XA SF software packages.

DISC DRIVES INC. Operations Manager/Systems Programmer. 3/77 to 6/83.

Directed a three-shift operation in a DOS/VSE environment on an IBM 4381. Areas of responsibility included Computer Operations, I/O Control and Distribution, managing the activities of 12 people on the staff. Directly responsible for all systems programming activities, including:

The installation and support of DOS/VSE SIPO 1.4.2, as well as tuning and DASD space management.

Installation of MSA Payroll and Human Resources System.

Installation of an IBM System 36 and related software components, and linked it to the mainframe for both 3270 and RJE support, to service the payroll application.

Operations Supervisor

Directed the activities of 3 Computer Operators, a tape librarian, and 3 I/O control clerks in a three shift operation. Developed logs and procedures to ensure completion of all scheduled work. Developed standardized, documented scheduling procedures. Responsible for training all new personnel.

Lead Computer Operator

Responsible for training new operators and distribution personnel. Reviewed all work produced and resolved all problems.

PROFESSIONAL ATTRIBUTES

I am a person who knows Technical Services from the ground up. I understand its importance in keeping a growing company productive, and take pride in creating order in the chaos of Technology.

Telecommunications Analyst

James Sharpe
9 Central Avenue
Jericho, NY 11753
(516) 555-1212

OBJECTIVE:

Challenging opportunity as Telecommunications Analyst.

SUMMARY:

Seven years progressive experience providing network analysis, system planning, product evaluation and selection. Comprehensive and cost effective installation, troubleshooting and maintenance of voice and data communications systems.

COMMUNICATIONS KNOWLEDGE:

Bell System, PBX's, Modems, MUX's and Fiber Optics. Specifically, Northern Telecom SLI, NEC NEAX 2400, Dimension 200, Rolm CBX, Mitel SX200, Strombergh Carlson DBX 1200/5000, GTE PIC, PCM Fiber Optic System, Equinox Data Switch and Tl. Functional understanding of Packet Switches, WAGNET and ETHERNET.

EXPERIENCE:

A MAJOR BROKERAGE/FINANCIAL CORPORATION: TELECOMMUNICATIONS ANALYST

Project manager for the planning and implementation of a nationwide voice and data communications network. Included development of a multi-side RFP to replace fourteen phone systems. Issued RFP's to vendors, conducted evaluations according to formats and configurations. Network design and traffic engineering using ETN networks. 1985 - Present

VIACOM, MANHATTAN: TELECOMMUNICATIONS VOICE/DATA ANALYST

Responsibilities included planning and implementing telecommunications for headquarters and field offices. Included long range requirements, new products and software releases, and recommending upgrades as required. reviewed and evaluated proposals, selected systems, assisted in system software design, and supervised implementation. 1983 - 1985

CHASE MANHATTAN: TELECOMMUNICATIONS ANALYST

Responsibilities included: Coordinating installation for international data communications networks in Europe and Africa. Reviewed company's product usage, and provided recommendations for effective use of data switches or data through PBX. Assisted in the selection and implementation of data switch (RS-232) for a CM subsidiary. 1981 - 1983

EDUCATION: 1984.   B.S. Telecommunications. (New York University)

REFERENCES: Available upon request

Textile Designer/Stylist

JANE SWIFT, 9 Central Avenue, Phoenix, AZ 85020. (602) 555-1212

Textile designer/stylist with 14 years experience in the apparel and home furnishing industries. I have developed management skills in the areas of creative development, merchandising and manufacturing.

SUMMARY

MERCHANDISING   In Jack Winter Ltd., I utilized my skills as a textile designer in the apparel market by producing moderate-priced garments within a vertical structure. I organized a company to merchandise, produce and distribute finished goods throughout the U.S. and Canada. Worded closely with department and specialty stores. Sales volume in three years grew from 0 to $1,500,000.00 a year.

DEVELOPMENT   As designer for Continental Textiles, worked closely with prominent textile printers in U.S. and Italy. Designed both the fabrics and the finished products for an untapped market. Organized a manufacturing and marketing force to produce and distribute products throughout the U.S. Commitments for the first season of business amounted to $1,000,000.

MANUFACTURING   Experience working for manufacturers of both volume and limited distribution. Developed technical skills and knowledge of a wide range of production methods. I have done business with numerous printers as well as subcontractors throughout U.S.

WORK EXPERIENCE

JACK WINTER DESIGNS, INC.   **1983-Present**
Custom designed printed and hand painted fabrics for interiors. Worked with major decorations and displayed in Kips Bay Decorator Showhouse.
    Pierre Deux, Inc.
    Designed major collection of decorative fabrics and wall-coverings. Most successful sales growth to date in its category.

CONTINENTAL TEXTILES, INC.   **1980-1983**
Textile designer/stylist for wholesale manufacture of luxury home furnishing products and loungewear. Worked closely with mills in Kentucky and Italy.

JACK WINTER LTD.   **1976-1980**
Designer, manufacturer of moderate price printed fabric and fashion apparel. Wholesale distribution across the U.S. in major department and specialty stores.
    Smithsonian Museum, Philadelphia Art Museum, Minneapolis Art Institute
    Designed and manufactured fabricated products for catalogues and gift shops.

MODERN TEXTILES INC.   **1973-1976**
Textile designer/stylist. Worked closely with mills and apparel designers. Moderate price sportswear.

references available upon request

Ultrasound/Nuclear Medicine Technician

Jane Swift
9 Central Avenue
Bellevue, WA 98007
(206) 555-1212

JOB OBJECTIVE: To utilize my knowledge and experience in non-invasive cardiology to provide the highest quality examinations possible.

EMPLOYMENT:

Bellevue Medical Center, Bellevue WA. 1985 - present. Chief Nuclear Medicine.
Nuclear medicine procedures, including:
SPECT, gated heart studies, thallium, programming and operation of nuclear computing systems. Responsible for development of procedures and protocols. Perform ultrasound procedures including abdominal, gynecological, and small parts.

Beaverton County Hospital, Beaverton OR. 1982 - 1985 Ultrasound/Nuclear Technician

Performed nuclear medicine and ultrasound procedures, instigation of the ultrasound department. Management of the two departments under the supervision of the chief technologist. Marketing new technology and procedures to staff physicians.

EDUCATION: University of Tennessee at Memphis
                  B.S. Nuclear Medicine Technology
                  School of Medicine
                  Certificate in Ultrasonography

SOCIETIES: Society of Diagnostic Medical Sonographers
                  Society of Nuclear Medicine

Underwriting Typist

Jane Swift
9 Central Avenue
Norcross, GA 30092
(404) 555-1212

SUMMARY

A professional with over nine years of full-time insurance experience, I started in the business, part-time, at 16. My employment and on-the-job training have given me a solid grounding on the agency and company side of Insurance. Having worked with underwriters and raters, I possess a complete understanding of underwriting guidelines and rating abilities on all lines of commercial coverages. It is my desire to continue my growth within the administration side of this industry

EMPLOYMENT EXPERIENCE

May 1979 - Present

Hartford Insurance Company, Norcross, GA
Underwriting Typist

Type insurance policies and endorsements, IBM 3180 CRT usage. Documents are typed using IBM Memory 100 typewriter. Basic office machines are utilized - copier, calculator, etc. Trained in Cancellations, Experations, Quotes and State Filings Departments.

January 1978 - March 1979

Southern Supply Inc., Norcross, GA
Secretary to President and Vice-President. One person office. General duties - answering phone, typing and filing. Compiled weekly man-hours for payroll.

References

References will be provided upon request.

Veterinary Intern

Jane Swift
9 Central Avenue
Englewood, NJ 07631
(201) 555-1212

EDUCATION

DVM - New Jersey State University, 1986
BS - State University of New York, Southampton
Currently completing MS in Poultry Science of NJSU.

EMPLOYMENT

School of Veterinary Medicine, NJSU. Avian Medicine Intern (1986 to present)
Involved in avian medicine research and field service areas of the NJSU School of Veterinary Medicine.

*Assist in the instruction of veterinary and undergraduate students.
*Diagnostic workup of avian cases at the Animal Disease Diagnostic Laboratory of the Department of Agriculture.
*Extensive co-op work with private poultry companies in New Jersey and other states.

School of Veterinary Medicine, NJSU, Research Technician (1983 to 1986)
Responsibilities include:
*Management of experimental sheep, swine, horses, and cattle.
*Collection of blood, urine, and feces for determination of clearance rates for a radioactively tagged anthelmintic.

Department of Poultry Science, NJSU Farm Manager (1981 to 1983)
Responsibilities include:
*Weekend management of turkey research unit including care and feeding of birds, egg collection, and hatchery management.
*Collection and analysis of tissues and data, performance of various electrolyte and hormone assays.
*Assistance in endocrinology laboratory instruction.

VETERINARY SCHOOL ACTIVITIES
*Freshman Class President
*Student representative to the NJSU Outstanding Teacher Selection Committee
*Student representative to the Ethics in Veterinary Medical Education Symposium, Knoxville, TN

PROFESSIONAL ASSOCIATES
*American Veterinary Medical Association
*American Association of Avian Pathologists
*Association of Avian Veterinarians

Visual Merchandising Specialist

Jane Swift
9 Central Avenue
Manhasset, NY 11575
(516) 555-1212

With twelve years' experience in Visual Merchandising Management, I have successfully:

* Coordinated all Visual Merchandising in Macy's third most profitable store.

* Supervised visual aspects of a successful $3 million store renovation with responsibility for new fixturing and merchandising.

* Conducted seminar in Visual Merchandising for all new department managers in Macy's eastern region.

* Utilized innovative image control techniques which contributed to a new high fashion store's becoming the volume leader for its entire chain in one year.

RECENT ACCOMPLISHMENTS

Visual Merchandising Manager of a Macy's store with a $40 million sales volume, I coordinated fixturing, merchandizing, and seasonal changes for all (12) departments along with responsibility for overall store image.

* Analyzed stock levels to determine new fixture needs, prepared requirement reports, and coordinated on-time deliveries of all fixtures.

* Reporting directly to the Vice President for Corporate Visual Merchandising, I supervised five Visual Merchandising Managers brought in from other stores to assist in the project.

* Interfaced with both union and non-union construction personnel while directing movement of departments under construction.

* Guiding all Department Managers through renovation and construction, I familiarized them with new fixturing and applicable merchandising techniques.

EARLIER ACCOMPLISHMENTS

As District Display Director for Laura Ashley Inc., a 100-store specialty women's ready-to-wear chain I developed fashion awareness, coordinated displays and trained staff, including new District Display Directors throughout the country. Reporting directly to the Corporate Display Director, I was:

* Given responsibility for image control at the company's new flagship store on 57th St, where fashion image was crucial. My innovative merchandising and display techniques contributed to this store's becoming the number one volume store for the entire company by its first anniversary.

* Recognized for my planning, organizing, and coordinating abilities, I was involved in several new store openings throughout the U.S and Canada.

As Display Coordinator/Visual Merchandising Manager with ESPRIT, Inc., I progressed to having a five-store responsibility. Developing my functional skills, I was promoted to Visual Display troubleshooter for a multi-state region.

EMPLOYMENT

MACY'S, 1981 - Present
LAURA ASHLEY, 1977 - 1981
ESPRIT DE CORPS, 1973 - 1977

EDUCATION

A graduate of Harper College, Palatine, Illinois, with a specialty in Fashion Design, I have also completed intensive course work in Architectural Technology which has significantly contributed to my expertise in store renovation and floor plan know-how. Course work in photography has rounded out my background.

PERSONAL

Interests include apparel design and construction, sketching and free-hand drawing.

Wholesale Electrical Salesperson

JAMES SHARPE
9 Central Avenue
Rock Island, IL 61204
(309) 555-1212

Sales/Sales Management
Administration..Distribution..Advertising

Versatile, goal-oriented sales professional with wide experience in sales, marketing and training. Expertise includes start-up/turn-around sales operations, increasing sales and new product/market development. Heavy exposure to advertising, outlet management, pricing, distribution, merchandising and sales analysis.

CAREER HIGHLIGHTS

SALES: As inside sales and quotation specialist, I contributed $3,000,000 of the company's $30,000,000 annual sales.

MARKETING: I improved by 25% a territory that was in the beginning stages of economic crisis in an oil-related economy.

COMMUNICATIONS: I created and developed the Chicago Chapter of the Illinois Electric League Man of the Year, 1982.

PROJECT MANAGEMENT: Conceived and implemented systems and procedures to increase sales territory from $1,500,000 to $2,000,000.

NEGOTIATIONS: As manager of the California branches of a multi-store electrical supply chain based in Mississippi, I negotiated purchases of special materials for promotion and sales effort. I also negotiated large-job material purchases up to $1,500,000.

PROMOTION: I conceived and directed in-house "tent shows", "open house" and regional "trade shows", to promote our chain throughout Midwest. Chairman Greater Chicago Electric League Trade Show Attendance Committee.

COMPUTER: Established systems for handling $600,000 in materials through stock each month, reducing overhead by 4.5%.

WORK HISTORY

Large Electrical Distributor	Chicago, IL 1985-Present
Lake Lighting & Supply	Sacramento, CA 1983-1985
Stern Electrical Sales	Brownsville, TX 1980-1983
Top Supply	Chicago, IL 1980-1981
Metro Electric Supply	Chicago, IL 1979-1980

ADDITIONAL PROFESSIONAL TRAINING

Dale Carnegie Sales course
Dale Carnegie Public Speaking and Leadership course

EDUCATION

Extensive credits from University of Michigan, University of San Jose and Duke University.

Word Processing Specialist

JANE SWIFT
9 CENTRAL AVENUE
LEXINGTON, KY 40579
(606) 555-1212

EXPERIENCE:

January 1982 - present
Word Processor. Corporate Headquarters of a national company.

Currently working on an OIS/140 system that involves editing, creating and printing of corporate budgets, memos, a variety of charts, letters and telecommunications. I also assume all of the Supervisor's responsibilities in her absence.

January 1980 - January 1982
Data Librarian/Scheduler. Kentucky Turf Club, Lexington, KY.

Included the control, input and output of data tapes. Prepared a processing schedule and coordinated all input and output to meet objectives of schedule. Responsible for preparing a morning report to management, accounting for all variances from the prior day's processing schedule, and assisting in problem determination and resolution.

March 1975 - January 1980
Data Entry Operator/Senior Operator. Kentucky Turf Club

Started with the company as a data entry operator and after 6 months was promoted to senior operator. In early 1978 the data entry staff was cut to only myself which gave me full responsibility for all turnover of data entry and maintaining a schedule on the priorities of the work.

September 1973 - March 1975
Data Entry/Senior Operator. Blue Mountain Telephone Co., Lexington, KY.

Trained with Blue Mountain Telephone Co. during a work study program in high school and went on to the following companies as a data entry operator and was soon promoted in each to Senior Operator: Lexington Glass, Manny Kerber P.C, and Kentucky. Auto Rating Bureau.

HARDWARE EXPERIENCE:

IBM-047, 029, 059, 129, 3741
Apple Mac II, SE, Plus
Decision Data - 8010
WANG OIS/140

EDUCATION

Wang Laboratories Inc. - 1987: Administrative Course
Computer Associates - 1985: Tape/Disk Management
IBM-1975: 3741
Lexington Business School - 1970: Data Entry

References available upon request

Word Processing Supervisor

Jane Swift
9 Central Avenue
Milwaukee, WI 53201
(414) 555-1212

EXPERIENCE:

6/87 - Present: **Richfield and Simon, Wilwaukee, WI**. Word Processing Supervisor

* Prioritize and distribute workload for operators on several shifts in a forty-attorney law firm.

* Manage and supervise day, evening, and weekend word processing center on OIS-140 system.

* Thorough knowledge of all word processing advanced functions, utilities, glossaries and telecommunications.

* Interview, hire and evaluate word processing operators.

10/76 - 6/87 **National Cardboard Company, Milwaukee, WI**

6/83 - 6/87 Supervisor/Coordinator - Word Processing Operations

* Supervised and maintained Wang OIS-140 systems for several departments. Duties included: Solving and correcting general equipment problems, and monitoring capacity, library usage and loading software.

* Coordinated activities of word processing operators for three centers. Created glossaries to aid operators in formats and styles. Devised instruction and reference manuals with easy-to-understand language.

* Trained personnel in equipment operation and maintenance.

* Liaison with Wang Laboratories' Software and Customer Engineers.

* Consulted with and performed trouble-shooting and maintenance for operators in other departments in the company.

10/76 - 6/83 Administrative Assistant to the Director of Investor Relations.

* Researched market and financial data, communicated daily with security analysts, and handled highly confidential information.

5/74 - 9/76 **1st National Bank, Milwaukee, WI**

Administrative Assistant/Systems Assistant Supervisor - Research Department

Assisted Security Analyst in compiling statistics and information for research reports. Assisted Systems Supervisor in supervision of IBM Mag Card operators and secretaries.

EDUCATION: * Numerous development courses.
* Various training courses at Wang Laboratories.

REFERENCES: Will be furnished upon request.

Appendix

Resumes for Special Situations

Off The Beaten Track

For more help...

Sample Questionnaire

Resumes for Special Situations

These are resumes that performed above and beyond the call of duty for job seekers whose background didn't "fit the mold." They're invaluable guideposts in presenting your own experiences in the most flattering light.

Jane Swift, 9 Central Avenue, Tampa, FL 33614. (813) 555-1212.

SUMMARY OF BACKGROUND

Varied business experience in both public and private sectors, with particular expertise in Human Resources Management, Sales, and Other Management areas.

EXPERIENCE

Human Resources Management/Counseling

-Set up Personnel Department and acted as Director for rapidly expanding marketing company, with responsibility for recruitment of staff at all levels, establishment of policies and operating procedures, compliance, wage and salary administration, and employee relations.

-Worked in alcohol detoxification and counseling program in municipal hospital setting. Handled voluntary, referred and involuntary cases. Provided short-term intervention, longer range treatment planning and individual support whenever needed.

Management

-Managed retail sales operation, with responsibility for hiring, training, directing and evaluating employees. Set and maintained inventory policies, with involvement in purchasing, warehousing, display and stock handling.

-Performed quality assurance and inspection functions within manufactuing operations. Involved in laboratory testing of incoming stock and materials in process.

-Purchased and expedited parts for major defense manufacturing operation, working against critical deadlines. Dealt with a number of vendors and internal sources.

Sales

-Accountable for increasing and developing new via referral, advertising, merchandising, and calling. Assisted customers in determining nee product presentations and completed sales tran Performed all relevant customer service functi

Jane is a recovered alcoholic re-entering the work force.

Jane Swift, 9 Central Avenue, Tampa FL 33614. (813) 555-1212.

EMPLOYMENT
1965 to present

James Cathedral - Tampa
Sexton

Gulf Shipping - Miami
Researcher, Manifests

Kinko's - Ft Lauderdale
Personnel Director

Ocala Medical Center - Ocala
Counselor

Industrial Plastics Inc. - Ft. Myers
Quality Control Inspector

Penney's - Ft. Myers
Salesperson

Infarking Laboratories Inc. - Ft. Myers
Quality Control Inspector, Lab Technician

Chubb Life Insurance Co. - Ft. Myers
Salesperson

Lockheed Aircraft - Sunnyvale, CA
Parts Expediter

AFFILIATIONS

Personnel Management Association
Central Massachusetts Employers Association
U.S. Army - honorably discharged

EDUCATION

Ft. Myers Community College
-A.A. Counseling minor: Education, 1976
-graduated magna cum laude

James Sharpe
9 Central Avenue
Aurora, CO 80014
(303) 555-1212

OBJECTIVE A challenging position providing an opportunity to apply broad Management experience.

EDUCATION University of Colorado
MBA program - presently enrolled
B.S. Public Administration, Colorado College

QUALIFICATIONS Progressively responsible management background in a large medical facility, with successful experience in the following areas:

Staff Supervision - presently responsible for 30 skilled, semi-skilled, unskilled and managerial employees. Hire, train, direct, and evaluate the staff. Responsible for their output and the quality of their work. Maintain morale, motivation and positive employee relations. Solve problems, take corrective action, apply company policy.

Operations Management - direct staff and activities in several support departments, including maintenance, grounds and buildings, laundry, housekeeping. Manage a budget of nearly a half million dollars. Schedule all departments for the most effective use of manpower, equipment and facilities.

Inventory Control/Purchasing - maintain an inventory control system for non-medical supplies and food.

Other - frequent involvement in customer and public relations, promoting the facility; work with other staff to prepare for licensing, compliance reviews; involved in Real Estate Management - buying, renovating and maintaining rental properties; licensed in real estate sales.
As public administration Intern at both the state and federal levels, involved in labor relations activities, legislative actions, communications.

EMPLOYMENT
1982 to present Aurora Rest Home, Aurora, CO
Supervisor - promoted from Assistant

1978 to 1982 Coors Brewery, Golden, CO
Construction Worker

1976 to 1978 Intern - federal and state

James has changed careers many times.

Jane is a handi-capped worker who wants to change careers.

Jane Swift
9 Cental Avenue
Monroe, WI 53566
(608) 555-1212

OBJECTIVE Seeking a challenging position in Customer Service.

SUMMARY -Possess a combined Customer Service and Financial background. Responsible for administering several aspects of pension plans. Significant customer service responsibilities as Office Manager and Credit Coordinator.

QUALIFICATIONS

-Present position requires accuracy and efficiency in creation of files, calculation of benefits and options, analysis of IRS qualification, preparation of tax forms, and other similar activities.

-Effective verbal and written negotiations with agents, attorneys, plan participants, accountants and others. Good communications skills are necessary for confidential inter-departmental communications.

-Experience includes Credit and Office Management. My responsibilities in credit include taking applications, securing credit approvals, ordering products and arranging for delivery. I also calculated salespeople's commissions. As Office Manager, I handled customer service duties, accepted and booked payments, maintained inventories, and performed other functions associated with keeping the office running smoothly.

EXPERIENCE
1969 to present

BC/BS
Pension Technical Specialist

Sears
Credit Coordinator - for major appliances

3M Products
Office Manager

Big Brothers/Big Sisters; United Cerebral Palsy Assoc.
(6 years, part-time)
Office Manager/Clerical

```
                    James Sharpe
                    9 Central Avenue
                    Claremont, NC 28610
                    (704) 555-1212

OBJECTIVE        An opportunity to apply technical skills and
                 communications ability in a Sales or Customer Service
                 position.

SKILLS SUMMARY   Thoroughly familiar with the process of quoting and
                 producing industrial products for a wide range of
                 customer applications. Work with customers'
                 specifications, ideas or blueprints to produce parts on a
                 special or stock basis. Call on accounts to assist with
                 product development, to provide service in the event of
                 discrepancies or quality questions. Duties require the
                 ability to communicate effectively on technical problems,
                 and to establish rapport.

                 In a retail setting, have held major responsibility for
                 staff supervision and customer service, managing several
                 functions with high customer and employee contact.

                 As a supervisor, held responsibility for training,
                 scheduling, directing and evaluating the work of skilled
                 machinists. Keep areas of responsibility supplied with
                 tooling, materials and equipment to ensure the most
                 effective use of manpower and machinery.

                 Acted as buyer of industrial products: drills, reamers,
                 slotting saws, collects, high-speed carbide steels,
                 ceramics, lubricants, NC screw machine programs, among
                 others.

                 Operated and troubleshot sophisticated machine shop
                 equipment, including Swiss screw machines, grinders,
                 lathes, milling machines, drill presses. Able to program
                 CNC equipment. Conversant with the full range of machine
                 shop practices, quality and production control
                 procedures.

EXPERIENCE       Jig Tools, Claremont, NC
1980 to present  Supervisor, Quality Control Inspector
                 Production Machinist.

1979 to 1980     Finest Foods, Raleigh, NC
                 Front End Manager, supervising an eve
                 Involved in cashiering, packing, cred
                 cashing.

1974 to 1979     Atlas Moving Co., Raleigh, NC
                 Truck Driver, Mechanic

PERSONAL         References available upon request.
```

James is a blue-collar worker who wants a white-collar job.

Jane has had multiple jobs and needs to combine her experience.

```
                    Jane Swift
                    9 Central Avenue
                    Kenner, LA (504) 555-1212

OBJECTIVE        A challenging Sales or Sales Management position,
                 providing an opportunity to apply broad experience and a
                 record of success in marketing a variety of products and
                 services.

QUALIFICATIONS   Sales - Thoroughly familiar with techniques for
                 generating new business in industrial, commercial and
                 consumer markets. Employed cold call, referral and other
                 prospecting techniques. Skilled at assessing client
                 needs, making effective sales presentations, often
                 involving technical product details.
                 Have regularly exceeded sales quotas.

                 Sales Management - Responsibilities included selecting,
                 training, motivating and supervising professionals in
                 sales, service, and other operations.
                 Performed market research and promotions, forecasting,
                 the development of distribution systems, and other
                 marketing administration functions.
                 Developed marketing plans, arranged financing, helped
                 establish distribution networks.

EMPLOYMENT       ADT Systems - Worcester, MA
                 Commercial Sales Representative  1986 to present

                 Patriot Marketing - Worcester, MA
                 Owner/Consultant  1984 to 1986

1974 - 1984      Maxxum Industries, Inc.
                 Self-Employed Restaurateur
                 Cherry Buick
                 Goodnick Miller
                 International Harvester

TRAINING         Studied Business Administration, Management, and
                 Marketing at Louisiana Institute of Technology, the
                 University of Texas, and Kenner Junior College. Have
                 received technical product and sales training in numerous
                 courses and seminars throughout my career.

PERSONAL         U.S. Navy - honorably discharged

                 References available upon request
```

James Sharpe, 9 Central Avenue, Huntsville, TX 77340. (713) 555-1212.

OBJECTIVE	Personnel Management
SKILL SUMMARY	PERSONNEL - Staffed and managed several organizations, developing policies and programs emphasizing employment, job development, vocational assessment and training:

- Screened, selected and hired professional and para-professional staff. Developed personnel policies.
- Devised testing, vocational assessment and job skills counseling programs. Conducted skills and job search training. Extensively screened candidates.
- Sought and secured job opportunities. Negotiated for the placement of referred candidates. Conducted extensive follow-up activities to ensure the success of placements.
- Reviewed job proposals, studied applicable wages and structures, and performed detailed analyses of required worker traits, job functions and occupational trends.

PLANNING - As director of several agencies, devised a number of service programs to meet community needs:
- Planned long-range, intermediate and daily activities. Reported on results within the confines of policy, law, budget and deadlines.

COMMUNICATIONS - Maintained close liaison with staffs of agencies at the local, state and federal levels, including a consortium of seventeen cities and towns.
- Generated contacts in the business community to locate job openings, to obtain or provide information about programs and to provide follow-up.

BUDGETING - Prepared staff, resources and activities budgets ranging in size from $100,000 to over six million dollars. Researched costing, historical data and relevant economic factors. Determined sources and availability of funds.
- Negotiated with various agencies to gain approval for funds. Ensure that proposals were made according to applicable procedures and regulations.
- Developed reporting, monitoring and control techniques, identifying variances and taking corrective action when necessary.

MANAGEMENT - Accountable for purchasing, security and supervision of facilities. Participated
number of political campaigns, with resp
activities as recruiting, polling, canva
research, staff supervision and others.

EMPLOYMENT	Judge Paul Zamudio Institute of Human Re
	Director 1980 to present
	Town of Huntville
	Public Service Employment Director 1979
	Janus Projects, Inc. - Houston
	Planner 1978
	Community Advocacy Probation Project - H

James is an ex-convict looking for his first job out of prison. (Much of his experience was gained on work-release programs.)

Career Change: Pension Specialist to Human Resources Worker.

Jane Swift
9 Central Avenue
Rockville, MD 20852
(301) 555-1212

OBJECTIVE	Opportunity in Human Resources/Benefits/Compensation/Recruiting.
QUALIFICATIONS	Extensive supervisory experience, managing administrative details of pension plans on behalf of corporate and individual clients. My responsibilities have required skills in several areas, including:

Financial/Analytical
Administrate details of pension plans ranging in size from 1 to 2,500 participants. Thorough knowledge of plan design, funding practices, benefits, taxation and disclosure. Supervise the systems and people who gather detailed pension data, conduct analyses, and report on valuations, benefits, tax information, reporting requirements.

Communications
Successfully employ written and oral communications skills when dealing with clients, their accountants and attorneys, actuaries, in-house technical experts, field offices, and government agencies. Responsible for timely and accurate preparation of a wide array of reports and filings.

Supervision
Direct a small staff. Assisted in their selection. Responsible for training, supervision, evaluation, and motivation. Ensure that the flow of work is smooth and that all deadlines are successfully met. Responsible for problem-solving, and handling difficult or unusual cases. Able to manage and coordinate multiple projects simultaneously.

EXPERIENCE	Maryland Life Assurance Company
	Rockville, Maryland
1976 to present	Pension Specialist, Group Pension Services
EDUCATION	B.S. Education, 1975
	Vassar
PERSONAL	Willing to travel, relocate

```
                James Sharpe
                9 Central Avenue
               Minneapolis, MN 55440
                 (612) 555-1212
OBJECTIVE        A challenging position in Security Management, providing
                 an opportunity to apply extensive technical and
                 supervisory experience.

SUMMARY OF       -Thoroughly experienced in a wide range of security
BACKGROUND       situations. Physical protection of persons, property and
                 facilities; intelligence gathering, investigations, other
                 related applications.

                 -Responsible for:  Active and passive security of
                 documents, personnel, facilities (under routine, hostile
                 and combat conditions); use of agents; intelligence
                 activities; biological, nuclear and chemical security;
                 protection of large facilities, airfields and explosives.

                 Experienced in the penetration of other security systems;
                 intrusion and surveillance devices; documentation
                 control; iIENCE
                 United States Army, Special Forces
1983 to present  Command Sergeant Major, managing training programs in
                 security
1980 to 1983     Chief Instructor - providing training in security and
                 community living to personnel overseas
1977 to 1980     First Sergeant, Headquarters Company - training and
                 deploying Special Forces involved in security
1967 to 1977     Intelligence Sergeant - providing security, training,
                 utilization of agents and physical security in hostile or
                 combat situations.
```

After spending over 25 years in the military, James is returning to civilian life.

Career Change: Medical Technology Worker to Salesperson.

```
                 Jane Swift
                9 Central Avenue
                Utica, MI 48087
                 (313) 555-1212
OBJECTIVE        An opportunity to apply Medical Technological background
                 in a challenging Sales or Marketing position.

QUALIFICATIONS   -Over six years experience in Medical Technology in
                 hospital laboratory and outpatient settings. Have worked
                 successfully with physicians in a number of disciplines,
                 including pathology, geriatrics, oncology, other areas;
                 interact daily with laboratory staff (supervisory and
                 technical), patients, and other people throughout the
                 hospital.

                 -Thoroughly familiar with complex, sophisticated
                 laboratory equipment, such as Coulter S plus IV, Coulter
                 550, MLA 700, Fibrometer. Provide technical training to
                 other operators, and Medical Technology students.
                 Accountable for the accurate calibration of equipment,
                 basic troubleshooting and maintenance.

                 -Maintenance of inventory, purchase of supplies, and
                 quality control procedures in general.

                 -These duties require a person who is thoroughly
                 knowledgeable about laboratory and highly technical
                 equipment and associated procedures, is familiar with
                 materials, and is precise in performance of duties.

EMPLOYMENT       Utica Family Hospital - Utica, Michigan
1982 to present  Special Hematology Laboratory Technologist, promoted from
                 Laboratory Technologist.

EDUCATION        B.S. Medical Technology, 1982
                 Detroit State College (Detroit, Michigan)

                 Registry eligible in Hematology

                 Additional training by laboratory equipment manufacturers

REFERENCES       Excellent professional references are available upon
                 request.
```

James Sharpe
9 Central Avenue
Dallas, TX 75231
(214) 555-1212

SUMMARY

Expert in bicycle freestyling. Starting in 1985 at the age of 10, I've developed my skills to the point where I'm a regular participant in demonstrations, parades and shows, a winner in several competitions, and I've been asked to appear on TV, in magazines, and in commercials.

Shows

Since June of 1986, I've been a member of the Stuntsters Trick Team (sponsored by Athlete's Foot). Both individually and with other team members, I've been in more than 20 shows throughout Texas. Some of these are paid appearances, some provide premiums, and others are done as a courtesy.

Competitions

In statewide meets, competing against others in my class and in higher classes, I've consistently placed in the top 5. My specialty is the Flatland event. I'm presently competing on a national level. In addition to competing I've won awards for bicycle safety.

TV/Broadcast/Print

I've appeared in numerous TV news film clips, and in a "PM Magazine" feature. I was featured in a 30 second commercial spot for BMX bicycles, and recently completed filming a 30 second national TV spot for Snapple. "Rad Zone" magazine, a national newsletter for the sport, will be featuring me in an upcoming edition. I'm now under active consideration for a part in a soon to be produced feature film.

Other Activities

When not practicing freestyling (up to 5 hours a day), I like to ski and surf. During the summer I work as a golf caddy.

A complete potfolio is available for inspection.

James is only fourteen years old!

Jane is a recently divorced homemaker who wants to re-enter the workforce.

Jane Swift
9 Central Avenue
Wichita, KS 67218
(316) 555-1212

OBJECTIVE

An entry position in Personnel or Human Resources Management, providing an opportunity to apply formal education in the field, and business experience.

EDUCATION

Anna Maria College - Paxton, Massachusetts
B.A. Psychology
Graduated magna cum laude

SUMMARY OF SKILLS

Studies have included courses in Industrial Psychology, Personnel Management, Marketing, Management, Accounting, other Psychology and Liberal Arts courses.

Experience in Interviewing/Communications, gained from extensive dealings with customers, clients, students, and peers in the organization. Capable of effective written and oral communications where the ability to gather precisely and act on it is critical.

Background in Counseling, with both adults and students in academic and professional settings. Assisted with Career Counseling and other forms of personal assistance.

Experience includes work as a Telemarketing Representative, as an Administrative Assistant. Have held leadership positions in volunteer organizations, including Chairman, Fundraiser, Advisory Board Member, and Counselor. Duties have required the ability to organize, set up and implement systems for getting tasks completed, the ability to be persuasive and obtain cooperation.

EXPERIENCE

Wichita Employment Services
Telemarketing Representative. Working from research, leads and cold calls, identify target markets and make over 500 sales calls per month. Provide quotes, and refer results of research for further action. Set up relevant sales administration systems.

1982 to 1986

Kansas State University
Worked part and full time while attending college.
Assignments included:
Secretary in the Graduate Office, in the Development Office, and to the Director of the Nursing Program.

ACTIVITIES

Chairperson, Boy Scout Troop Committee; Member, Advisory Board; Fundraiser, Counselor, Navy Officers' Wives Association; Fundraiser, Library Committee.

PERSONAL

Health: excellent
Willing to travel/relocate

James Sharpe
9 Central Avenue
Indianapolis, IN 46178
(317) 555-1212

OBJECTIVE   A challenging opportunity in the areas of Fundraising, Customer Service, or
             Sales

SUMMARY OF   A varied work and educational background, with experience in managing
QUALIFICATIONS people, coordinating projects, public relations, fundraising, and related
             activities.

             Fundraising
             Have successfully solicited from individuals, corporations and other
             organizations, securing goods and services. Contacted and communicated
             effectively with donors in the United Nations community (embassies,
             hospitals, others). Thoroughly familiar with person-to-person and telephone
             techniques. Hosted and coordinated events.

             Project Coordination
             Served as creative consultant to the Executive Director of the Foundation on
             "Save the Children" benefit event.
             Assisted with details of this fundraising campaign that netted over $600,000.

             Management
             Experience in warehouse management. Responsible for staff involved in
             receiving, storage, distribution, transportation. Established methods, stand-
             ards of performance and productivity. Maintained morale and motivation
             (World Hunger Foundation).

             Training
             Education includes college courses in Government, Public Speaking, Logic
             and related subjects. Certified Diver (Commercial Diving Center-San
             Francisco, California), with background in rigging, maintenance, salvage.
             Received military training (U.S. Marine Corps.) in motor transportation,
             reconnaissance, and food service.

PERSONAL   Military: U.S. Marine Corps - Vietnam era veteran

             During much of my life I've volunteered time and services, and have gained
             considerable skill in a number of occupational areas. I've developed a sense
             of initiative and empathy, am able to communicate effectively, and have
             demostrated a deep and practical commitment to others in need.

James is re-entering the workforce after being in a mental hospital.

Off The Beaten Track

Herewith, some of the more impressive resumes in employment areas you don't come across every day. Some of these fields may not seem to require a resume—at first glance. The fact is, virtually any position is competitive, even the unusual ones. The authors of these samples thought twice, set themselves apart from the competition, and picked up the jobs they deserved.

Jane Swift. 9 Central Avenue. Chicago, IL 60611. (312) 555-1212

Call me Top Gun.

A writer committed to excellence. A writer who wants to be the best. work with the best. learn from the best.

A Top Gun who's been around—especially around consumer and high-tech. Who's always reaching for breakthrough. And who's very, very fast.

I'm looking for an agency that's sincerely committed to outstanding creativity. One where my best work won't go through life as a comp.

What can I do for you? Write ads. radio. and TV spots that soar above the noise.

Produce AV and videos that perform up to promise. And back you up. whatever it takes.

If you need a Top Gun—a team player who knows tactics and reaches for the top—maybe we should talk. What we already share is a passion for excellence.

Let's schedule a check ride.

OBJECTIVE   *To be the best. work with the best. learn from the best.*

CURRENTLY
Senior Copywriter. Compton Burnett
Clients:
Dynatech ◆ Communications ◆ Dennison ◆ Augat Pylon ◆ Avanti Communications ◆ Corporation ◆ AFI/Datatrol Telesis ◆ Datel ◆ Amperex ◆ Advanced Technology ◆ Xyplex

1984-85
Account Executive. Foote Cone Belding. Set up Midwest branch of International Agency.
Clients:
Applicon ◆ Itek Graphics Systems ◆ BBN ◆ plus introduction of the Ricoh line of personal computers

1983-84
Writer/producer. Creative Services Source. Chicago: Film. video. radio and TV.
Clients:
Marathon Development ◆ Saunders & Associates ◆ The United Way ◆ Colibri ◆ Stanley Hardware ◆ Fram ◆ Key Microsystems ◆ Fleet National Bank

1979-83
Copywriter. Pierce Brown Associates. Rochester. NY
Clients:
Bausch & Lomb ◆ Corning Glass Works ◆ R.T. Company ◆ Citibank ◆ Telex ◆ Xerox

1969-79
Freelance writer. Worked extensively with Me Homes & Gardens)

EDUCATION   B.A. Duquesne University. 1968
Art direction. RISD. 1985

Copywriter

Mail Clerk

James Sharpe
9 Central Avenue
Houston. TX 77031
(713) 555-1212

EXPERIENCE

10/83 - present   **Gordon, Roffe, Sinclair (Houston, TX)**
Position: Mail/File Clerk

Duties: Daily upkeep of alpha-numerical, cross reference, domestic and international filing system; opening, organization and close-out of files; daily operation of Xerox machines; processing of daily incoming and outgoing mail, including operation of Pitney Bowes Postage Meter machines; inventory, ordering and stocking of supplies; general upkeep of file department.

11/78 - 3/83   **Boggs, Evans & Horn (Houston, TX)**
Position: Mail Clerk/Messenger

Duties: Processing of daily incoming and outgoing mail, including operation of Pitney Bowes Postage Meter machines; distributed interoffice material; operation of Xerox machines. Operation of the Kodak Ektaprint Copier Duplicator. Transmission of Telex & Telex copy messages.

EDUCATION

1978 - 1979   **LaGuardia Community College, NY**
Major: Accounting

References will be provided upon request

Jane Swift, 9 Central Avenue, Baltimore, MD 21201. (301) 555-1212

CAREER OBJECTIVE
To pursue a career in OB/GYN, with a sub-specialty in Fetal Maternal Health, with an opportunity to combine my interests in Surgery and Internal Medicine. I expect to seek board registry in both OB/GYN and in Internal Medicine.

EDUCATION

Carte School of Medicine - University of Maryland
Doctor of Medicine — 1983

University of Maryland
M.S. Pharmacology — 1981
B.A. Biology, cum laude — 1979

PROFESSIONAL TRAINING

St. Joseph Medical Center - Baltimore, Maryland
Internal Medicine Residency Program (Level II) — 1985
Categorical Internship, Internal Medicine — 1984

The Memorial Hospital - Baltimore, Maryland
Internal Medicine Residency Program (Level III) — 1985
OB/GYN Elective

University of Maryland Medical Center - Baltimore
Gynecology Elective — 1986

HONORS AND AWARDS

National Honor Society — 1974-76

Carter School of Medicine - Biomedical Research Symposium
First Prize, Medical Student Category — 1981
First Prize, Best Paper in Oncology — 1981

St. Joseph Medical Center
Award, Outstanding Intern of the Year — 1983-84

PRESENTATIONS PUBLICATIONS

Eastern Student Medical Research Forum - Presentation. — 1981

"Regulation of Mitogen Response and Erlich Ascites Tumor Growth by Miconzone". (Abstract)

"Effect of Arachidonic Acid and Prostaglandin Hemolytic Plaque Formation". 1978. (Abstract)

ACTIVITIES

University of Maryland Pre-Med Society Treasu
Eastern Student Medical Research Committee
Representative, University of Maryland
American Medical Association
St. Mary Medical Center Housestaff Associatio

Physician (Seeking Fellowship)

Plant Breeder

James Sharpe
9 Central Ave
Ft Lauderdale, FL 33339
(305) 555-1212

EXPERIENCE
4/81 - Present

SOUTHERN SEEDS - Ft. Lauderdale, FL
Research Director (1985 - Present) - Responsible for Citrus breeding activities in Florida and making product recommendations (canned, frozen, concentrates). Supervising one plant breeder, one technician and up to 20 hourly workers.
ACCOMPLISHMENTS:
-Increased the size of breeding and testing program by 50%;
-Identified superior Citrus products for a successful entry into the citrus market;
-Identified and developed superior citrus products to strengthen sales in all maturities;
-Provided product information to dealers and sales personnel in an understandable and concise form.

Plant Breeder (1981 - 1985) - Responsible for strengthening corn breeding and testing effort.
ACCOMPLISHMENTS:
-Improved mechanization of the citrus project;
-Initiated and developed the computerization of the citrus project;
-Increased size and scope of citrus breeding and testing by 100%, while introducing numerous frost resistant strains.

FLORIDA STATE UNIVERSITY - Tallahassee, FL
3/4 Time Research Associate (1/79 - 2/81)
-Researched the heritability of Citrus quality traits.
-Assisted in operation of citrus project including planting, harvesting, and data collection.
1/2 Time Research Associate (1/77 - 1/79)
-Researched frost tolerance in citrus.
-Assisted in operation of citrus project including planting, harvesting, and data collection.

EDUCATION
1981
1978
1975

PhD. Plant Breeding - Florida State University
MS. Plant Breeding - Florida State University
BS. Agronomy - University of Minnesota

Respiratory Therapist

James Sharpe
9 Central Avenue
Warminster, PA 18974
(215) 555-1212

SKILL SUMMARY:

Respiratory Therapist familiar with Bennett, Sechrist, and Bear respirators (Adult and Infant), intubation, arterial blood gas sampling, transcutaneous monitoring, polysomnographic monitoring, transport techniques, and electrocardiography.

EXPERIENCE:

1985
to
Present

Critical Care Respiratory Therapist
Warminster Children's Hospital, Warminster, PA

Responsible for all aspects of infant critical respiratory care, plus routine respiratory patient care. Serve as an alternate shift supervisor, supervising four persons.

1978
to
1985

Staff Therapist
Veterans Memorial Hospital, Philadelphia, PA

Worked as a Staff Therapist beginning 1980; was responsible for intensive and general respiratory care hospital-wide.

EDUCATION:

Worked as a Therapist Assistant while in school, responsible for routine respiratory care in non-critical areas. Funded all educational costs.

1978   A.S., Respiratory Therapy, University of Oregon

1976   B.S., Biology, University of Oregon

CERTIFICATION:

Certified Respiratory Therapy Technician (CRRT) by NBRC
Registered Respiratory Therapist (RRT) by NBRC

REFERENCES:

Available upon request.

T.V. Installation Specialist

James Sharpe
9 Central Avenue, Apt 45
New York, NY 10019
(212) 555-1212

OBJECTIVE — Seeking an opportunity to apply my skills and experience in Cable TV installation/construction.

QUALIFICATIONS

- Experienced in all phases of cable TV installation and construction. I've worked on residential and commercial installations, in urban, suburban and rural areas.

- Working individually or as crew chief, I've handled all kinds of installation projects, ranging from very simple to complex, both pre-finish and post-wire, in single or multi-family dwellings and high rise buildings.

- My skills include blueprint and schematics reading, inside and outside wiring, finish plastering, painting and carpentry, drilling through concrete and flexcore, excavation, and cable testing.

- I serve as the company's troubleshooter, handling special projects as well as difficult or time consuming installations, where technical skills, customer relations and problem-solving ability are very important.

- In previous jobs, I've worked construction, remodeling, mechanical repair, and TV repair.

EXPERIENCE
1986 to present

Gotham Cable, New York
Installer

1984 to 1986

Trump Construction, New York
Siding and Roofing sub-contractor

1984

Gray Construction, Brooklyn
Concrete Worker

1983 to 1984

Heavy Hauler Inc., Bronx
Diesel Mechanic, promoted to Bookkeeper.

PERSONAL

Health: excellent
Open to relocation

References and a portfolio with photos of my recent jobs are available.

Trades Supervisor

James Sharpe
9 Central Avenue
Campbell. CA 95008
(408) 555-1212

QUALIFICATIONS
-Experienced Electrician. with twelve years in job-site supervision (Foreman. General Foreman. Electrical Coordinator). Licensed in California and Arizona. Have studied electrical engineering. and attended a number of electrical foreman seminars. Member. IBEW Local 356 since 1976.

-Supervised the entire electrical operation for a major contractor on a variety of projects including: Schools. fire stations. hospitals. colleges. restaurants. office building, housing for the elderly. municipal buildings. correctional facilities. and other similar jobs.

-Responsibilities have included supervision and training of crews (electricians—apprentices and journeymen. as well as foremen). Coordinating electrical requirements of the job with all other subcontractors (fire protection. HVAC. plumbing, equipment installation). Ordering and expediting of materials; dealing with inspectors. general contractors and other project officials.

-Accountable for total control of all electrical aspects of the job. requiring day to day supervision. quality, safety. employee labor relations.

-Experienced on a wide variety of projects. from simple system updates to the most complex jobs, taking them from ground level to final completion.

-Communicate effectively on a daily basis with architects. engineers and other on interpretation of drawings, design modification. and problem solving.

-Consistently bring in projects at or under budget.

EMPLOYMENT
1978 to present
Electrical Coordinator. General Foreman. Foreman
Valley Electric - Burlingame. CA

1971 to 1978
Journeyman Electrician
M. Johns (Detroit). Barry and Jones (New Yo[rk] (Worcester. MA). Western Electrical (Flagstaf[f] Brothers (Los Angeles).

Woodcrafts Specialist

James Sharpe
9 Central Avenue
Memphis, TN 38137
(901) 555-1212

SUMMARY OF BACKGROUND
- Qualified wood craftsman and artisan, with formal training in woodworking, sculpture, and photography.
- Business experience includes opening and operating a sawmill, creating and selling custom wood products, designing and producing furniture, home restoration, cabinetry, other similar work.
- Developing and producing woven products.

TRAINING
- U. T., Tennessee School of Fine Arts
  Bachelor of Fine Arts, 1973
- Studied Woodworking, Sculpture, and Photography in this jointly-run program.

- Apprentice to Bernard Pennymaker (furniture designer) of Memphis for five years.

EXPERIENCE
1983 to present
Craftsman/Sawmill
Sole proprietor of a multi-faceted business: a sawmill, precision woodworking shop, supplier of specialty lumber to various industries, design and production of custom products, both on commission and for sale.
- Personally responsible for all creative and administrative aspects of this business.

1978 to 1983
Pennymaker Woodworking - Memphis
Sole Proprietor of this sawmill and woodworking shop.
- Quarter sawn lumber was the specialty. Projects included: custom designed furniture, building of spiral stairways, cabinetry, sawmill operations.

PERSONAL
Health: excellent

REFERENCES
- Business, personal and customer references, as well as samples. photos and sketches are available, and will be gladly shown upon request.

For more help...

The following individuals and corporations are leaders in their chosen fields. They each donated considerable time and energy to contributing to the quality of this book. They are the people on the firing line of the corporate hiring game. If you are a professional seeking professional career advice, you will be wise to seek advice from them. If they can't help you directly, they will point you in the right direction.

Automotive

Dale Boch, President, Management Developers, 687 Highland Ave., Needham, MA 02194

Territory: New England

Specialization: Auto Dealer recruiting and consulting

Banking

Joy Porrello CPC, President Dunhill of Northeast Tulsa, 10159 E. 11th St, Ste 370, Tulsa, OK 74128

Territory: National

Specialization: President, CFO, Controller, Auditors, Compliance Officer; CLO, Trust Officer, Operations Officer, Loan Officers, Cash Management, Loan Review, Training, Compensation, etc.

Computers

Mike Badgett
President
Dunhill of Cherry Hills Village, 2950 South Jamaica Court, Suite 300, Aurora, CO 80014

Territory: National

Specialization: Major specialization in UNISYS Computer Professionals. Operations, Programmers, Systems Analysts, Systems Programmers, Tech Support, Programming Managers, Technical Management.

Debra Fox, President, Fox Inc., 1401 La Grange Street, Chestnut Hill, MA 02167, 617/469-3400

Territory: New England

Specialization:
Telecommunications: Voice and Data, Hardware and Software, Marketing and support. Software Engineering. Data Processing: MIS, Applications and Systems Development.

Alan Daum, President, Dunhill of Dublin, 4900 Blazer Parkway, Dublin, OH 43017, 614/766-3612

Territory: Eastern half of U.S.

Specialization: Software engineers in the mini and micro areas, and process control engineers.

Mike Zarnek, Al Katz, Chuck Szajkovics, 1st Search, 4200 W. Peterson, Suite 100, Chicago, IL 60646, 312/282-8810

Territory: National

Specialization: Telecommunications, from executive to engineering levels.

Ralph Owen, President, Kiley-Owen Associates, 1218 Chestnut Street, Suite 510, Philadelphia, PA 19107, 215/923-0740

Territory: United States, Europe, South America, Japan, Canada

Specialization: Data and Telecommunications, and Software Management.

Marvin Bearman, President, Ronald Cohen, Sr. Vice President, Dunhill at Tower Place, 3340 Peachtree Road, NE, Suite 2570, Atlanta, GA 30026, 404/261-3751

Territory: National

Specialization: Hardware and Software sales. Also subspecialties in Healthcare, Trust Banking, Engineering and Office Personnel.

Food Service

Jim Fowler, President, Dunhill of Huntsville, 2010 Jordan Lane, NW, Huntsville, AL 35816

Territory: National

Specialization: Sales and Marketing, Research and Development, and Technical Services in Food service and all Agribusiness Industries.

Graphics

Kelly Clark, Partner, Alden & Kelly, 643A Tremont Street, Box 167, Boston, MA 02118, 617/247-1147

Territory: New England

Specialization: Freelance Mechanical Artists.

Healthcare

Jim Tipton, HealthCare Recruiters, 8323 S.W. Freeway, Suite 800, Houston, TX 77074

Territory: National

Specialization: Sales Professionals in the Healthcare, Pharmaceutical and related fields.

Pat Erickson, Dunhill of Shawnee Mission, 7801 West 110th Street, Suite 103, Shawnee Mission, KS 66210-1311, 913/451-8333

Territory: National

Specialization: Healthcare (and Banking professionals).

Dawn Hiner, President, Medicall, 2401 Fountain View, Suite 510, Houston, TX 77057-7578, 713/783-7600

Territory: National

Specialization: Physicians, Nurses, Administrative and Technical Personnel for hospitals, clinics, home health agencies, laboratories and research institutions.

Legal

Elizabeth Gillard, President, Gillard Associates, 850 Providence Highway, Dedham, MA 02026, 617/329-4731

Territory: National

Specialization: Attorneys of all disciplines.

Office Support

Anne Sweidall, President, Sweidall Associates, 446 Main Street, Worcester, MA 01608, 617/755-3424

Territory: Central Massachusetts

Specialization: Office Support, Administration, Word Processing, Accounting and Finance. Also temps.

John Winn, President, 5950 Fairview Road, Three Fairview Plaza, Charlotte, NC 28210, 704/553-0050

Territory: North Carolina

Specialization: Office Support Services.

Ray-Jean Fellows, President, Grove Personnel Services, Opus West II, 1411 Opus Place, Suite 118, Downers Grove, IL 60515, 312/968-2771

Territory: Downers Grove and Chicago

Specialization: General Office Staff, Administration, Legal Administration, Word Processing, Quality Control, Insurance

Cynthia Steinmetz, Forum, 342 Madison Avenue, NY, NY 10017, 212/687-4050

Territory: Manhattan

Specialization: Legal and General Office Support Staff, Word Processors.

Ann Binder, President, Ambassador Personnel, Inc., 14 Granite Street, One Parkingway Building, Quincy, MA 02169

Territory: Greater Boston

Specialization: Administrative Assistants, Executive Secretaries, Word Processors, Office Managers, Customer Service Representatives; Paralegals, Sales Assistants, Bookkeepers, Researchers, Typists, Receptionists, Management Trainees, etc.

Resume Creation

Jeff Hunter, President, First Impressions, 72 Cambridge Street, Worcester, MA 01603, 617/755-8311

Territory: Within personal reach of the office in Worcester

Specialization: Resume creation.

Joan Willing, Future Search, 280 Guy Lombardo Ave, Freeport, N.Y. 11520. (516) 867-6998

Territory: Nationwide

Specialization: Resume creation

Sample Questionnaire

This sample questionnaire was filled out by a fellow professional using the question-naire guidelines on pages 28-34. Actual resume examples based on the following information—chronological, functional, and combination formats—can be found on pages 73-77.

1. Current or Last Employer:
This includes part-time or voluntary employment if you are a recent graduate or about to re-enter the work-force after an absence. That does not mean you should ignore this section: Try looking at your school as an employer and see what new information you reveal about yourself.

```
BRANCH MANAGER
Starting Date   11/78
Starting Salary  $13,000
Leaving Date   8/80
Leaving Salary  $26,000

AREA MANAGER
Starting Date   8/80
Starting Salary  $31,200
Leaving Date   11/83
Leaving Salary  $41,600

DIVISION MANAGER
Starting Date   11/83
Starting Salary  $62,400
Leaving Date   3/85
Leaving Salary  $62,400
```

2. Write one sentence that describes the products your company made or the services it performed.

```
BRANCH MANAGER through DIVISION MANAGER:
MICRO/TEMPS sold software consulting services to the computer user
industry.
```

3. List your starting job title (the one given to you when you first signed on with the company). Then write a one or two sentence description of your responsibilities in that position.

```
BRANCH MANAGER
Started a new division of the Technical Aid Corporation called MICRO/TEMPS.
Was responsible for developing a client and applicant data base, while
showing a profit for the division.

AREA MANAGER
Opened an additional office in the Washington area. Was accountable for the
profitability of both the Boston and Washington offices.

DIVISION MANAGER
Responsible for market studies for future branches to be opened. Directly
involved in choosing new locations, opening office, training staff and
having the office profitable in less than one year's time.
```

4. What were your three major duties in this position?

```
BRANCH MANAGER
A)  Selling software services to clients.
B)  Interviewing applicants and selling them on consulting.
C)  Setting up interviews for applications and clients to meet.
```

AREA MANAGER
A) Training sales and recruiting staff.
B) Developing and implementing goals from forecasts.
C) Interfacing with other divisions in order to develop a working relationship between different divisions.

DIVISION MANAGER
A) Hired and trained Branch Managers for all new offices.
B) Developed P & L forecasts for the B.O.D.
C) Developed and implemented division policies.

5. Now, for each of the above three duties, answer the following questions:

What special skills or knowledge did you need to perform this task satisfactorily?

BRANCH MANAGER
A) Knowledge of the computer industry.
B) Key contacts in the Mass. computer industry.

AREA MANAGER
A) Knowledge and experience developing a branch.
B) Experience training sales and recruiting staff.

DIVISION MANAGER
A) Knowledge and understanding of developing a profitable division.
B) Knowledge and experience hiring and training branch managers.

What has been your biggest achievement in this area? (Try to think about money saved or made, or time saved for the employer. Don't worry if your contributions haven't been acknowledged in writing and signed in triplicate, so long as you know them to be true without exaggeration.)

BRANCH MANAGER
Successfully developed a new division of the Technical Aid Corporation. Now generating $18,000,000 in revenues.

AREA MANAGER
Successfully opened new branches for the division and hired and trained the staff.

DIVISION MANAGER
Built division to $20 million in annual sales.

What verbal or written comments were made about your contributions in this area, by peers or managers?

BRANCH MANAGER
Hard-working, stay-at-it attitude

AREA MANAGER
Hires good people and knows how to get the best out of them.

DIVISION MANAGER
Her division always makes the largest gross profit out of any of the divisions.

What different levels of people did you have to interact with to get this particular duty done? How did you get the best out of each of them?

BRANCH MANAGER
A)   Superiors - Listened to their ideas and then tried to show them I could implement them.
B)   Co-workers - Shared experiences and company goals--set up some competition.
C)   Subordinates - Acknowledged their responsibilities as very important for the team.

AREA MANAGER
A)   Superiors - Explained situations clearly and made them understand our options.
B)   Co-workers - Challenged to reach goals.
C)   Subordinates - Complimented when and where it was necessary.

DIVISION MANAGER
A)   Superiors - Asked for the experience and advice in difficult situations.
B)   Co-workers - Set up and accepted contest between managers.
C)   Subordinates - Made them feel they were extremely important as a member of the team.

What aspects of your personality were brought into play when executing this duty?

PERSONALITY: BRANCH MANAGER TO DIVISION MANAGER
strong will-power
stick-to-it attitude
high achiever
aggressive
high goal-setter

6. If you asked for a promotion or a raise while in this position, what arguments did you use to back up your request?

BRANCH MANAGER - Increase in sales.

AREA MANAGER - Increase in responsibility.

DIVISION MANAGER - Increase in gross profit and responsibilities.

7. Write down your current (or last) job title. Then write a one or two sentence description of your responsibilities in that position, and repeat steps 3 through 6.

Current title - Personnel Manager

Step 3:   Description of responsibilities. Hiring all internal staff of technical managers and sales people, additionally responsible for hiring all external consultants.

Step 4:   Three major duties:
    A)   Hiring of all internal & external consultants
    B)   Setting up wage and salary guidelines
    C)   Establishing the Boston office so it could become profitable quickly

Step 5:   Skills or knowledge needed:
    A)   Ability to source qualified candidates
    B)   Experience in start up situation
    C)   Knowledge of the Boston marketplace

Biggest achievement: Helped in making the branch profitable in nine months.

Verbal or written comments: A no-nonsense kind of person, aggressive and
      hard-working; good at getting the best out of people

Superiors: Was up front with any problems and clearly and concisely laid
out all the alternatives.

Co-workers: Set up good networking of communications to have information
flow quickly and easily.

Subordinates: Made them aware that we all had a lot to do, but that we
were all important.

Step 6: Raise or promotion.

Increase in sales figures and was responsible for hiring more
consultants then we had originally discussed.

8. Make some general observations about work with this employer.

   Looking back over your time with this employer, what was the biggest work-related problem that you had to face?

They wanted to grow rapidly, but didn't want to invest the money it took to
recruit and attract good consultant talent.

   What solution did you find?

Got consultants through Boston Computer Society and other related
organizations and set up a very aggressive referral program.

   What was the result of the solution when implemented?

We started to attract quality consultants and our name was beginning to
circulate.

   What was the value to the employer in terms of money earned or saved and improved efficiency?

Company did not spend a lot of money on recruiting efforts and was able to
attract quality people.

   What was the area of your greatest personal improvement in this job?

Made many key contacts in some excellent organizations.

   What was the greatest contribution you made as a team player?

Brought internal staff members closer together as a working team.

   Who are the references you would hope to use from this employer, and what do you think they would say about you?

Ken Shelly. He was one of our first external consultants hired. He
would probably say that I identified some key consultants for this
project at Sheraton, and that he could always rely on me to help him
no matter what. Dave Johnson-he was our technical Manager. He would
say that I did my job extremely well considering the little resources
I had, and that I identified many quality applicants. He would also
say that I knew how to find even difficult people.

OTHER BOOKS BY MARTIN JOHN YATE
AVAILABLE AT YOUR LOCAL BOOKSTORE

Knock 'em Dead With Great Answers to Tough Interview Questions

Will you have the answers when the recruiter asks: Why do you want to work here? What can you do for us that someone else cannot? How much money do you want? Why do you want to change jobs? In Knock 'em Dead, Martin John Yate gives you not only the best answers to these and scores of more difficult questions, but also the best way to answer — so that you'll be able to field any tough question, and get the job and salary that you deserve. Don't leave your success to chance! Get Martin John Yate's best-seller book, Knock 'em Dead with Great Answers to Tough Interview Questions, 4th edition, 6x9 inches, 204 pages, paperback, just published, $6.95.

Hiring The Best

Contrary to popular belief, not all managers are mystically endowed with the ability to hire the right people. Interviewing is a skill that must be developed, and Martin Yate shows just how to identify the person who provides the best "fit" for any given position. Includes sections on interviewing within the law and hiring clerical help, as well as prewritten interview outlines. 6 x 9 inches, 204 pages, paperback, $9.95.

ALSO OF INTEREST . . .

The Job Bank Series

There are now 18 *Job Bank* books, each providing extensive, up-to-date employment information on hundreds of the largest employers in each job market. Information includes contact person, address to send resumes to, phone number and company description. Most listings include common professional positions, educational backgrounds sought and even fringe benefits offered. Recommended as an excellent place to begin your job search by *The New York Times, The Los Angeles Times, The Boston Globe, The Chicago Tribune,* and may other publications, *Job Bank* books have been used by hundreds of thousands of people to find jobs.

Books available: *The Atlanta Job Bank —The Boston Job Bank —The Chicago Job Bank —The Dallas Job Bank —The Denver Job Bank —The Detroit Job Bank —The Florida Job Bank — The Houston Job Bank — The Los Angeles Job Bank — The Minneapolis Job Bank —The New York Job Bank —The Ohio Job Bank — The Philadelphia Job Bank —The Phoenix Job Bank — The St. Louis Job Bank —The San Francisco Job Bank —The Seattle Job Bank —The Washington DC Job Bank.* Each book is 6 x 9 inches, over 250 pages, paperback, $12.95.

If you cannot find a book at your local bookstore, you may order it directly from the publisher. Please send payment including $2.75 for shipping and handling (for the entire order) to: Bob Adams, Inc., 260 Center Street, Holbrook, MA 02343. Credit card holders may call 1-800-USA-JOBS (in Massachusetts 617-767-8100). Please first check at your local bookstore.